PATTERNALIA

Patternalia

AN UNCONVENTIONAL
HISTORY OF POLKA
DOTS, STRIPES, PLAID,
CAMOUFLAGE, & OTHER
GRAPHIC PATTERNS

JUDE STEWART

BLOOMSBURY

NEW YORK · LONDON · OXFORD · NEW DELHI · SYDNEY

Bloomsbury USA
An imprint of Bloomsbury Publishing Plc

1385 Broadway	50 Bedford Square
New York	London
NY 10018	WC1B 3DP
USA	UK

www.bloomsbury.com

BLOOMSBURY and the Diana logo are trademarks
of Bloomsbury Publishing Plc

First published 2015

ISBN: HB: 978-1-63286-108-5

Library of Congress Cataloging-in-Publication Data
has been applied for.

A catalogue record for this book is available from the
British Library.

2 4 6 8 10 9 7 5 3 1

Designed and typeset by Oliver Munday
& Taylor Goad
Printed and bound in China by RR Donnelley Asia
Printing Solutions Limited

To find out more about our authors and books visit
www.bloomsbury.com. Here you will find extracts,
author interviews, details of forthcoming events and
the option to sign up for our newsletters.

Bloomsbury books may be purchased for business or
promotional use. For information on bulk purchases
please contact Macmillan Corporate and Premium
Sales Department at specialmarkets@macmillan.com.

For Seth (Again)
& Lev

Contents

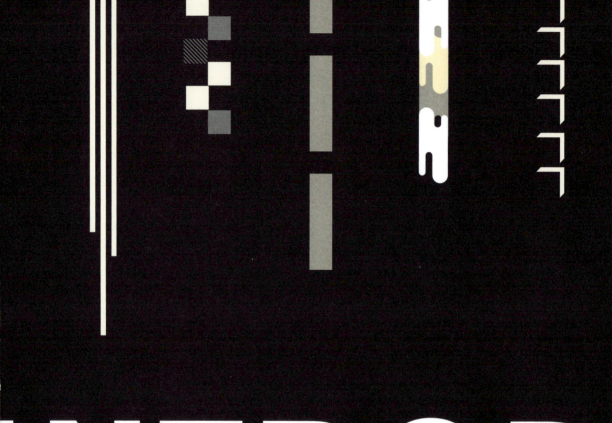

INTROD

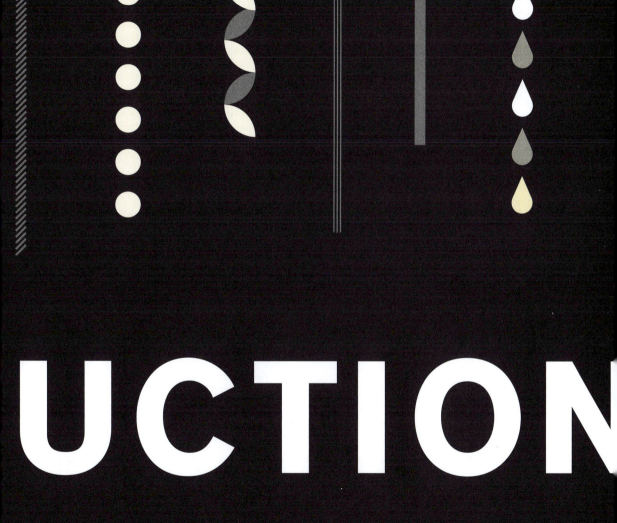

UCTION

Why a book on patterns?

Man is a complex of patterns, or processes. We speak of our circulatory system, our respiratory system, our digestive system, and so it goes. Man is not weight. He isn't the vegetables he eats, for example, because he'll eat seven tons of vegetables in his life. He is the result of his own pattern integrity.

—R. Buckminster Fuller, *I Seem to Be a Verb* (1970)

Seen or unseen, patterns proliferate. Wake up and blearily part the <u>stripes</u> of your Venetian blinds, then pad your bare feet along the whorls of wood-grain flooring to arrive at the breakfast table. Still bumbling, you pour a bowl of <u>honeycomb</u> cereal: a sweetly floating simulacrum of the kingdoms constructed by bees. The kitchen tablecloth is <u>gingham</u>, redolent of summertime and the prairies. (Why? How?)

Select today's outfit. The clothes arcing behind you are all bedecked in patterns: <u>seersucker</u> pants, paisley-strewn scarves, <u>polka-dotted</u> ties, camouflage T-shirts. The stuffed sock drawer explodes with patterns whose names you can recite automatically: argyle, herringbone, houndstooth, <u>fleur-de-lis</u>. Patterns are ubiquitous—and largely invisible. We often dismiss them as mere decoration.

Yet patterns aren't just pretty abstractions; they also gird up nearly every system in the natural world. Eddying water, flocking birds, <u>fractal theory</u> making cousins of lightning, stock prices, and the layout of African villages: All are explained by scientists and mathematicians by parsing

---

✒ <u>stripes:</u> Stripes convey speed, wit, prohibition, bloodiness, and spiritual completeness (among other things). See page 47.

■ <u>honeycomb:</u> Why are honeycombs made of hexagons? Turn to page 90.

■ <u>gingham:</u> Also known as "vichy," this simple pattern has achieved ubiquity in a stepwise fashion. See page 79.

✒ <u>seersucker:</u> For more, see page 53.

● <u>polka-dotted:</u> Turn to page 23.

✿ <u>fleur-de-lis:</u> Quite possibly the world's first blockbuster logo, cornered by the French for a solid millennium-plus. See page 103.

⌐ <u>fractal theory:</u> See page 125.

their underlying patterns. Pattern connects the cool, abstracted world of science to the feverishly meaning-mad world of people.

What makes pattern so persistently beguiling? Each pattern starts with an abstract formula: a figure, a plane, and a few rules about spacing, repeating or interconnecting the figures. Observed up close, it's a pleasure to unravel a pattern's signature, to reverse-engineer how it's made. Its ability to grow and grow—its whiff of infinity—is exciting. Yet as a pattern does grow, that sense of infinity alters. Writ large, a plane of surging dots or speeding lines seems to slow down, recede.

On a gut level, we imbue patterns with personality: demure polka dots, wholesome gingham, decisive stripes, fashion-plate houndstooth. And patterns can be potent. Take camouflage; or kaffiyeh, that distinctive check worn by Palestinian men as a headdress and by Brooklyn ironists as a scarf. Either pattern can unite a fighting force or stand out alarmingly in a hostile crowd.

To some, the existence of *any* pattern holds serious implications. In his 1908 essay "Ornament and Crime," Modernist architect Adolf Loos accuses pattern-slash-ornament of indulging savagery, prolonging imperialism, draining human vitality, weakening the economy, and blocking historical progress. Here's Loos: "Anyone who goes to [Beethoven's] Ninth Symphony and then sits down to design a wallpaper pattern is either a con man or a degenerate." And yet symphonies unfold according to a pattern, too—a fact Loos chooses to ignore.

Historians of textile or architecture often define pattern's meaning at a slant. For instance, paisley—the ornate shawl pattern originally worn by Mughal princes in India—is meaningful to those historians to the extent that it prompted the invention of the Jacquard loom, which dramatically reduced the time and cost of textile production. To the historian crowd, paisley *means* the foolhardy attempts to import Tibetan goats to Europe for their ultrafine wool; the sudden enrichment of weavers in Paisley, Scotland; a "paisley" encircling the shoulders of every Western shopgirl; and a century-long economic bubble. Paisley's actual visual stamp goes unread.

This narrow lens ignores all the other meanings crowded in paisley's amoeba-like shapes. Under its original name, *boteh*, paisley abstracts the shape of a lotus, a cypress, a leech, a mango, a date palm, and a dragon, each endowed with symbolic powers. Illiterate farmworkers in India watched for the signal that harvest work had begun: a curled fist, stamped in ink and then pressed against a wall, a hand-paisley. Somehow paisley became the uniform of prim grandmas, dazed-and-confused hippies, and (via sweat-soaked bandannas) American cowboys and gay men cruising for sex. From each group paisley accrued meanings, lore, conflicting stories and associations. We literally wear these stories on our backs—and we haven't yet begun to read them.

"The ephemeral is not the opposite of the eternal," art critic John Berger wrote in his 2008 book *From A to X: A Story in Letters*. "The opposite of the eternal is the forgotten." The buried stories of polka dots, paisley, and stripes verge on the forgotten, but they deserve the searching

3

● fashion-plate houndstooth: Also a favorite pattern of British hunters and coke-addled chefs. See page 79.

■ camouflage: Camouflage isn't only meant for hiding. It's also about being seen: confusing the eye, subverting reality, asserting identities. See page 109.

■ kaffiyeh: For the many kerfuffles over kaffiyeh, turn to page 84.

■ paisley: See page 95.

● bandannas: See page 102.

excavation we give any topic that's pervasive, eternal, and deeply compelling.

Patternalia is a popular cultural history of graphic patterns, from stripes to polka dots, from camouflage to fleur-de-lis, and many less familiar ones. This book plumbs the backstories of individual patterns, the surprising kinks in how each developed, the uncanny parallels (and overlaps) between patterns natural and invented, and the curious personalities patterns develop over time.

Patternalia aims to bushwhack its way across established topics, to wreak havoc on hierarchical categories of knowledge, to open your eyes to how many different things a simple pattern can mean—across cultures, disciplines, time periods, and contexts.

How to Read This Book

Imagine you could enter not a keyword into Google search, but a wordless image—say, a snippet of pink-and-white polka dots. What are this pattern's far-flung cousins? What surprising stories intersect behind this simple visual?

This happens to be the subject of chapter one, "Dots & Spots." To medieval Europeans, irregularly spaced dots signaled skin disease and moral uncleanness. Dots of various kinds sizzle across Bushman rock-art, suggesting different kinds of supernatural potency. The pattern Westerners call "polka dots" got its name from the peasant dance craze (and related merchandising mania) that took Europe and America by storm from the 1840s through the 1860s. But even as polka dots in the twentieth century became associated with the upbeat and innocent, they also channeled more sinister energies: Consider the evil comic-book character Mister Polka-Dot or the "girl in the polka-dotted dress," a minor but critical witness to Robert F. Kennedy's assassination in 1968.

Keyword searches turn out to be remarkably limiting. Searching the term "polka dots," you'd never discover many of its visual cousins like German *Thalertupfen*, the "dollar coin" print referencing the outmoded German currency from which our word "dollar" got its name. French *quinconce* would similarly elude you. The arrangement of dots seen on the five-side of dice, quinconce (in English, quincunx) tattoos have marked Russian prisoners, Vietnamese gangs, Portuguese patriots, traveling Romany, and Thomas Edison. A keyword search would give you nothing about Japanese *ensō*, a Zen Buddhist meditation in which one draws freehand circles to express one's evolving spiritual temperament, a process that fills reams of paper with what amounts to polka dots.

Much like traditional pattern-sample books, this book organizes patterns loosely by similarity of looks. You've gotten a taste of some of the tales contained in "Dots & Spots." "Lines & Stripes" reveals curious, untold stories of how a pattern we now find speedy, athletic, and wholesome was used by medieval European painters to tag disreputable characters like prostitutes and the insane. A stripe pattern also marked the Beast of Gévaudan, a Sasquatch-like creature that stalked the French countryside just prior to the French Revolution. Barber-pole stripes abstracted the

- skin disease and moral uncleanness: Turn to page 30.

- Mister Polka-Dot: See page 32.

- "girl in the polka-dotted dress": See page 28.

- quinconce: See page 35.

- ensō: More on page 34.

/ disreputable characters: The prohibition against stripes was stringent enough to land a bunch of thirteenth-century Carmelite monks in hot water. See page 47.

/ Beast of Gévaudan: Picture a ravenous Loch Ness Monster in an Enlightenment-era wig. See page 57.

/ barber-pole stripes: Includes bonus, dishy tidbits about famous barbers in nineteenth-century London. Turn to page 60.

bloodied bandages used by barbers in their original three services: hair-cutting, bloodletting, and tooth extraction. Finding a can of "striped paint" ranks among the fool's errands that tradesmen use to hoodwink new hires. In these tales and others, reading between stripes' lines reveals an evolving story of outcasts, subversion, sportiness, and sexiness.

Similarly, "Squares & Checks" explores the disparate meanings of simple black-and-white checkerboard (from auto-racing flags to an Indonesian cloth used as currency). It decodes well-known patterns like tattersall, zigzags, and plaid as well as less familiar checked patterns and motifs, like those in Ghanaian *adinkra* cloths. "Curves & Florals" provides deep-dive histories of three iconic patterns—fleur-de-lis, paisley, and camouflage—and introduces a trio of floral textile patterns that encode popular sayings and mottos. The book's final chapter, "Off the Grid," tells hard-to-pigeonhole stories about pattern drawn from science, mathematics, nature, and art. The chapter explores the more mind-bending principles of symmetry and chaos theory. To the chagrin (or relief?) of interior designers everywhere, mathematicians have determined there are only seventeen types of wallpaper patterns—that is, ways to tweak a repeating figure on a flat surface so you vary, but still preserve, the repeat. You'll find a global jaunt through pattern poetry and the meanings embedded in knot patterns. What mathematics can tell us about total patternlessness brings *Patternalia* full-circle, making it clear that patterns pervade the universe at every scale but

also, in a funny way, float above the world's fray, aloof and fantastical.

As you've likely noticed, *Patternalia*'s text is sprinkled with cross-references, so you can hopscotch across entries and patterns to follow an alternate storyline at will. Take the entry on the beast of Gévaudan, which offers readers a side door to learn about other animal patterns, like spotted panthers, which early Europeans likened to Christ and Uighur folklore cast as the bad guy in its version of Little Red Riding Hood. It goes on and (deliciously) on.

Patternalia is guided by whimsy yet grounded by a mission: to train an unexpected new lens on the world, the quietly revelatory one of pattern.

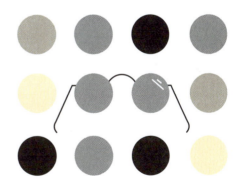

5

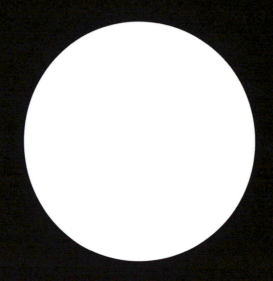

A Crash Course in Pattern:

The Basics

Pattern Lingo

At an imaginary cocktail party of pattern experts, you'd find two cliques with not much in common beyond a penchant for strange eyewear: designers and mathematicians. Below are some terms you'd need to mingle with each group successfully (and impress the paisley pants off everyone).

Start at the sparkling punch bowl, where designers are handing around silver cups of same. This group will warm up our pattern party, eventually passing the baton to the mathies. Designers with a yen for patterns tend to specialize in textile or wallpaper design, or the general category that includes both, *surface design*—that is, the creation of proprietary patterns that a corporate client can splash onto any surface, from smartphone cases to wrapping paper. Designers start patterns by choosing a *motif, figure,* or *unit*—all synonyms for the repeated element or subject of a pattern.

Next one chooses a *network* (also called a *grid* or *net lines*): a repeating combination of curved or straight lines, the (usually invisible) skeleton upon which a pattern is built. Let's imagine sketching a grid on a paper tablecloth next to the designers' punch bowl. The most popular networks are either a grid of *squares* (resembling a tic-tac-toe board) or *brick* (squares shifted such that the vertical lines between columns don't line up). A brick network turned ninety degrees is called a *half-drop.* A *diamond* network looks just like squares, but on a diagonal. A network of *triangles* will use equilateral triangles but not always. Networks of *hexagons* and *scales* evoke honeycombs and fish,

respectively. An *ogee* network completes this collection of grid types. Ogee lines are wavy; you can think of ogee as the gentler-proportioned cousin of the diamond or square pattern. Networks more complex than these are often built by dividing up a circle, a particularly rich trope in Islamic pattern-work. It's also possible to make a pattern's effect more complex by *interlacing* the figures and net lines. But this is only surface frippery: Peer past undulating details and the structure underneath should shine through.

Now comes *placement* of a figure onto a network, which defines the *interval* between figures. If the figures are crammed together, with little empty (or *negative*) *space* between them, the pattern might qualify as a *diaper.* (The etymological link between this kind of dense patterning and Junior's nappies isn't clear.) Diaper patterns appear frequently in backgrounds of medieval heraldic devices. As the female designers pat their lipsticked lips repeatedly on cocktail napkins, the interlacing figures (lips) produce an ersatz form of diapering.

Pattern designers also talk frequently of specific effects, like a *figure-ground reversal*: where the figure and background are equally sized and therefore easily confused with each other. (A chessboard or equally spaced stripes qualifies as a simple figure-ground reversal.) When you superimpose a second pattern on top of an existing pattern, that's called a *countercharge.* Some pattern effects relate to textile or printing processes, like *resist-dying,* in which you trace a pattern onto fabric with wax, dip the fabric in dye, then peel away the wax. (Other resist methods or *shibori* involve pleating, clamping, tying, or wrapping.) *Moiré* refers

---

■ **brick:** Know your soldiers from your shiners, would-be bricklayers. The lexicon of brick patterns starts on page 90.

■ **honeycombs:** "The Honeycomb Conjecture" is an Actual Math Thing and perfect conversational grist on any occasion. Turn to page 90 to learn more.

⌐ **Islamic pattern-work:** For a beautiful collision of geometry, decoration, and the sacred, turn to page 121.

⟋ **medieval heraldic devices:** See page 48.

⟋ **equally spaced stripes:** Figure-ground reversal might explain why medieval Europeans found stripes so scandalous. To tantalize your own eye, turn to page 47.

to overprinting of a pattern onto itself at a not-perfect angle, so the pattern appears to strobe. A pattern consisting of a gradually shaded single color has its own name, *ombré*.

By now the designers are deep in their cups, puppy-piling in an ecstasy of scarves. So let's swing wide the doors to our second group of pattern fans, the mathematicians. This crowd beelines it to the appetizer table, where they get busy arranging pigs-in-blankets to illustrate their own pattern lingo.

When geometricians (math types who specialize in geometry) think of patterns, they're most often concerned with the question of *symmetry*, or regularity of elements. Let's start with arranging those figures on a *plane*, à la the pigs-in-blankets on a paper plate. Spearing a toothpick into the center of the plate allows you to explore *rotational symmetry*. Picture two pigs laid directly across from each other, an inch away from a toothpick. Add another pig, and to maintain rotational symmetry you'd need to nudge the pigs to two, ten, and six o'clock, respectively, each an inch from the toothpick. The three little piggies are now symmetrically rotating around a central point, the toothpick, an example of 3-rotational symmetry. Rotational symmetries can climb higher in number the more pigs we add.

Reflectional symmetry happens when you introduce a line: Picture a celery spear laid horizontally on the plate. Figures (still pigs-in-blankets) will reflect themselves across the line, as if the celery were a mirror. Rotational and reflectional symmetries are collectively known as *point symmetries*, because each revolves around a fixed point.

You can also combine rotational with reflectional symmetry. Known as *dihedral symmetry*, that's when the lines of reflection intersect at a central point of rotation. A daisy's petals makes a handy illustration of a dihedral symmetry: Each long petal is a reflectional symmetry, and all the petals rotate around the flower's central point.

Patterns can also grow by *dilation*: the figures repeat identically, but grow larger or smaller along an axis. Dartboards, waves of increasing size, snail shells, and sunflowers all demonstrate dilation symmetries of different kinds.

That maxes out the basics of planar geometry, symmetry, and pattern. But if you're ready to hit the harder stuff, head over to the Advanced Patterns After-party on page 118. (That slightly twitchy egghead will show you the way.)

■ pigs-in-blankets: Also nice at a picnic. For the story of gingham, the classic picnic tablecloth pattern, see page 79.

Your Textile History Cribsheet

Patterns & Textiles: Like PB&J

Patterns have been spread across every possible surface: painted on rocks, shells, canvas, and pottery; carved into wood, clay, and marble; printed onto manuscript sheets, museum posters, and Phish T-shirts; and beamed out as screensavers and mobile phone wallpapers. But any history of patterns—even an unconventional one—bumps into textiles more often than any other surface.

Why? A few reasons. Textiles carry pattern in a format that's portable, therefore tradeable across oceans and steppes; they are historically tricky to produce, therefore rewarding of technological innovation; they are intimate because worn on the body. All of these factors made textiles a perfect vehicle for capitalistic product-lust and keeping-up-with-the-Joneses anxiety. Textile history is considered by many historians a fine proxy for the history of *all* industrial technology. One scholar argues that advances in textile production were "literally the software linings" of advances that drove the Industrial Revolution and our current era of "capitalism, speed, and abstract thinking."

To appreciate the stories of patterns most often associated with cloth—camouflage, paisley, plaid, gingham, the list goes on—it helps to feel conversant in the basic jargon and history of textiles. The following will equip you with convincing patter, should you stumble into a rabid knitting circle or a convention of textile historians.

Textiles 1-2-3

Setting aside animal-skin textiles, making most fabrics involves three steps: sourcing the raw fabric-stuff, turning it into a continuous thread, and then binding those threads into fabric. Adding color can happen after any of these steps, depending on the particular effect you're going for.

Step one—sourcing the raw material for fabric—can take myriad forms: gathering loose animal fur from shrubs, shearing an animal, gutting an animal and using its (cleaned-up) sinews, harvesting plant fibers or bark. Step one might also contain sub-steps to soften the fibers, like boiling, *retting* (breaking fibers down by moisture), sun-drying, or beating, as well as *carding* (combing to remove

B B
B B
B B

debris and align fibers in the same direction). Eli Whitney's cotton gin mechanized carding in 1794.

Step two, making thread, has often involved twisting. This super-simple binding method increases the thread's strength by diverting some of its tensile load into lateral pressure. Holding a supply of raw material on a *distaff*, you pull while twisting; the resulting thread gets wound around a *spindle*. In its simplest form, this is called *draft spinning*. You can spin thread just by rubbing fibers along your thigh or between your fingers, but a *spinning wheel* accelerates the pace considerably. (This gadget was invented between 500 B.C.E. and 700 B.C.E.) Multiple spinning wheels speeds things up still further, as does a mechanical power source. James Hargreaves' spinning jenny (circa 1764) produced a ton of thread with multiple spindles and hand power; Samuel Compton created more durable threads with more rapid machine power in 1779.

Sometimes you can skip step two if the raw material is already pliable and thread-like enough to manipulate. Felt, for instance, requires no thread-spinning. To make felt, first get some raw puffs of wool and degrease them. Second, knot the fibers permanently together. Two popular methods involve laying the fibers in cotton cloth, binding them tightly into a sausage, and then boiling it, or wetting the fibers with hot water and rolling them out, cookie-dough-like, between mats.

Step three—binding threads into a textile—was historically the slowest, most labor-intensive step and therefore a particular focus for innovators. Fabric gets made from scratch by weaving or knitting, or by a range of similar techniques like knotting, crochet, or braiding. In weaving, threads are generally held straight, whereas in knitting threads follow a meandering, looped path (called a *course*). Both weaving and knitting can be accomplished by hand or machine; we'll focus on weaving. The next section acquaints you with the three varieties of looms used in preindustrial weaving: backstrap, warp-weighted, and ground looms.

The Changing Anatomy of Looms

Loom lingo starts here. In weaving, one thread must stay taut: That's called the *warp*. The *weft* is the moveable thread whose action around the warp creates the weave. You hold the warp threads (called *ends*) tense between two *rods*, using weights or a convenient tree, or even a backstrap (a loom, one end of which is attached to your waist). You wedge a *shed rod* in between the warps to create a natural *shed* or opening for your *shuttle* or *bobbin*; your weft thread is wound around this doohickey and passed from left to right, or right to left, through the opening of the shed. Each pass creates a *pick* made of one weft thread. When one pick is in place the shed is opened up with the alternate configuration of warp threads, making room for the next pick.

The most boring weave, just endless weft-warp-weft-warp with zero variation, is cutely called *tabby*. If warp and weft are differently colored, you'd produce a basic plaid, but that's as fancy as tabby could get. To make fancier patterns you need a way to lift only certain warps, so you could weave just around the warps that remained flat. In basic looms, you could accomplish this by wedging in a *heddle rod*. You'd attach multiple warps to the heddle rod with loops, allowing you to raise and lower them as a group. Last but not least is the dramatically named *sword*, a rod used to beat the just-woven weft tightly into place.

Let's zero in on the heddles; those were the limiting factor in how complex patterns could get. You could add more than one heddle rod, and eventually the *treadle loom* allowed the weaver to manipulate heddles with a foot pedal. But a hand loom bristling with too many heddles got unmanageably crowded.

Enter the *drawloom*, now easily a millennium old. In a drawloom each warp was inserted through a *leash*, a network of cords suspended over the loom. First a "flower-lasher" programmed the drawloom manually. He read the pattern instructions detailed on graph paper and tied leashes into groupings, so warps could be raised or lowered together at whatever point the instructions called for. The harness cords in the ground weave could be similarly controlled. During weaving, a "drawboy" or "drawgirl" pulled the leashes to put the pattern's program into action.

A later innovation, the *dobby loom*, controlled all the warp threads with a peg arrangement. Dobby looms work hand-in-hand with another key innovation, the *flying shuttle*. As its name suggests, the flying shuttle zipped the weft thread more rapidly through the shed, making it easier, faster, and less laborious to weave textiles wider than arms' breadth.

Enter the *Jacquard loom*, a major textile game-changer. It automated drawboys out of existence and morphed the "flower-lashers" into "card-cutters." In the Jacquard loom all warp threads were controlled by two overhead series of joined punch cards. One set of cards determined the ground weave; the other replaced all the raisings and lowerings of warps the drawboy once handled. Uncannily futuristic, metal Jacquard cards look exactly like the paper punch-card "programs" guys in horn-rimmed glasses fed into room-sized computers in the 1960s.

Valerie Reilly, author of *The Paisley Pattern: The Official Illustrated History*, explains: "Following each line of the point-paper design, the cutter would use combinations of the ten keys on the machine to cut holes in the correct places on the cards. The cards were then laced into a continuous band and passed to the weaver ready for his machine." In other words, the one-time manual program produced by the "flower-lasher" was abstracted onto metal cards, one card per shuttle pass, that could be easily copied and reused. Reuse was totally the name of the game, too, as the upfront cost of making a set of Jacquard cards was steep: It took as many as 424,000 cards to program a single design. More than any other fear-provoking innovation, it was the dreaded Jacquard loom that prompted weavers to join Ned Ludd in 1812 in industrial sabotage, destroying wool and cotton mills under cover of darkness: the original Luddites. (Fun Sartorial Aside: The word "sabotage" derives from the French word *sabot*, or "clog." Luddites liked to chuck their wooden shoes into mechanical looms, breaking them in spectacular style.)

13

■ graph paper: Quad paper, isometric, logarithmic, or hexagonal? Who knew vanilla came in so many flavors? Read more on page 89.

Finishing a fully woven textile could involve a zillion other techniques, some of which introduced or altered the final pattern: braiding, quiltwork, appliqué, *fulling* (shrinking cloth to smooth its appearance), *waulking* (beating finished cloth to soften it), *cropping* (shearing excess threads, either from the front to create a velvet effect or from the reverse side), plus many others. In the preindustrial era, these tasks were backbreaking, repetitive, and dull. Scottish women, for instance, livened up the waulking necessary to finish <u>tartan</u> by beating the fabric in time to songs about love and heartbreak. (Too tired to give it your all? Just sit next to a woman recently wronged by her sweetheart and draft off her vim.)

Textiles Go Global

Luxury textiles had always traded globally, of course, but the Industrial Revolution accelerated and democratized this trade to a head-spinning degree. Machine weaving and knitting produced an abundance of cloth at ever-plummeting prices, with corresponding upheavals to the workforce and society. Textile printing techniques advanced, too, making it that much easier to stamp a pattern directly onto a textile's surface. (Textile printing made patterning so easy, in fact, it eventually gave rise to disposable fashions. More on these in the next section.)

■ <u>tartan:</u> Swooning nostalgia, fabricated history, three famous hucksters (two of whom were named James Macpherson).

The titillating history of tartan starts on page 72.

A pattern's meaning often wandered as it crossed national borders. An apt case-in-point are what's commonly known as "African prints," the gorgeously clashing, geometric prints scrawled with fat black lines, as if with Sharpie markers. This category of pattern is properly called Dutch wax batik, and its story shows just how many geographically dispersed meanings can embed in a given pattern.

The story starts in Indonesia, with a labor-intensive, handmade tradition of wax-resist patterning known as batik. Back when the country was called "the Dutch East Indies" in the nineteenth century, the Dutch colonial government enlisted West African slaves and mercenaries to beef up their military forces in Indonesia. Much like the Mughal paisley shawls sent home by French and British soldiers to their sweethearts, "Dutch wax batik" caught on in West Africa when these mercenaries traveled back home. Meanwhile, European textile manufacturers were intent on producing a cheaper, machine-made version of batik, with which they planned to flood the Indonesian market. But Indonesian consumers sniffed at early Dutch batik's imperfections: The machine-applied wax resist tended to crack, allowing dye to seep messily through. What Indonesians disdained as a design flaw, West Africans prized as unique—and, ever pragmatic, Dutch manufacturers started marketing batik in Africa instead. (Eventually Dutch manufacturers perfected the leaky wax-resist technique. But West Africans treasure the old imperfections so much, they're actually programmed into the designs now.)

Consumers in Togo, Ghana, and the Ivory Coast are aware of Dutch wax batik's complicated origins and love the pattern more because of them: They see Dutch wax batik as international and cosmopolitan. Today, West African consumers prefer European-produced prints—Netherlands-based Vlisco dominates the market—although an influx of cheaper Chinese batiks is making headway. A 2013 *Slate* article reported on how Vlisco is rallying by transforming itself into an international fashion house, employing couturiers and combative copyright lawyers. Vlisco plans to beat the Chinese by churning out a greater variety of patterns, although the Chinese are enlisting Togolese women to create even more designs—just like Vlisco and other Europeans once milked Indonesian craftspeople for pattern ideas. *Slate* sums up the company's conundrum and the dizzyingly layered history of this pattern: "The Dutch company that peddles Indonesia-inspired designs to West Africa may be edged out by the Chinese—and in search of a new market."

Patterns are just like passport stamps in the global-trade game: inevitably smearing as destinations accumulate.

Disposable Prints

Among the first "conversational prints"—textiles with patterns mechanically stamped on them—were *calico* and *toile de jouy* (or simply "toile"). Both originated as unbleached linen or cotton fabrics cheap enough to use as textile-pattern sketchpads. (To spare you wondering: The name "calico" is a corruption of *Kōlikkōdu*, known

15

● fat black lines: The
／ Asante people of Ghana
■ make another pattern, adinkra, that resembles a fat Sharpie grid filled with symbols meaning all kinds of things. For zigzagged adinkra, page 68; for checked adinkra, page 89; or adinkra featuring dots, page 38.

／ mercenaries: German soldiers-for-hire in the fifteenth century wore stripes, a future favorite for military insignia. For more on military stripes, turn to page 51.

♥ Mughal paisley shawls: See page 95.

● combative copyright lawyers: For litigators arguing heatedly against the originality of polka-dot designs, turn to page 24. Another lawyer professionally embroiled with dots: the one trailing dots-loving activist and artist Yayoi Kusama. See page 42.

to the British as *Calicut*, the city in southwestern India that for centuries produced the fabric.) *Toiles* now refer to any detailed illustration rendered as a pattern against a plain white fabric-stuff. While calicos stayed inexpensive and downmarket, toiles migrated upward: Think "French country house" or "whatever the Real Housewives of New Jersey doll up their breakfast rooms with." Toiles commemorated noteworthy events like the first balloon ascent or Queen Victoria's coronation in 1838. Contemporary toiles by the UK design firm Timorous Beasties show finely etched urban scenes of housing projects and strung-out junkies ignored by passersby glued to their mobile phones. "Calicos" now refer to tiny, cutesy patterns on sturdy fabric, appropriate for an apron print or a baby's coveralls. Because detailed calico prints read as splotches from a distance, "calico" also came to refer to multicolored cats and horses.

By the mid-twentieth century, patterns on disposable textiles reached their zenith with paper dresses. It all started with a 1966 mail-in campaign by the Scott Paper Company of Philadelphia. Consumers sent in a coupon from a Scott product plus $1.25, and in return they received a "Paper Caper" dress made of Dura-Weve, a new cellulose tissue reinforced with rayon and nylon that the company patented in 1958. Paper Capers came in either <u>red bandanna print</u> or a black-and-white Op Art pattern and moved like hotcakes: Scott distributed half-a-million dresses in just six months. Transience was core to their appeal: As Scott's sales pitch put it, "Won't last forever . . . who cares? Wear it for kicks— then give it the air."

From 1966 to 1968, both sides of the Atlantic bristled with more and more paper dresses. Lightweight, futuristic, affordable, and wipe-clean, paper dresses perfectly fit the moment's sartorial mood. They were sexy and customizable: Their flimsy appearance erotically suggested the body underneath, and they could be snipped ultra-short with scissors or colored with crayons. Like their descendant, the ironic T-shirt, paper dresses could be printed with everything from Campbell's soup ads to political candidates' grinning mugs to reprints of Allen Ginsberg poems. They fed consumers' insatiable hunger for new patterns—and when you got bored, you just crumpled and tossed the old dress and shook out a crisp new one.

Paper dresses also reflected all the ways the decade's mood soured. It got creepy to see advertisements rub off onto your bare skin. Overflowing landfills and growing eco-awareness made disposable clothes seem a lot less hilarious. Fending off spilled cocktails, lit cigarettes, and joints got old—and maybe dress-wearers got collectively more sloshed and sloppier. As one exhibit catalog put it: "Easy-care didn't necessarily mean easy-going." After 1968, paper dresses dwindled down to their current niche, disposable medical gowns, while their raw material lives on in FedEx mailers.

● <u>red bandanna print</u>: A curious afterlife of paisley in the New World. See page 102.

This Is Your Brain on Patterns

Gestalt Psychology

How do we perceive patterns cognitively—and why do we need to notice them at all? The answer starts in 1910 with Gestalt psychology (*Gestalt* means "shape or form" in German). In Gestalt terms, visually we crave *Prägnanz*, or "pithiness." Our brains like <u>symmetry</u>, orderliness, and simplicity—in short, pattern—so we use those principles to define whole forms in everything we see.

Gestalt laws of grouping describe how patterns reveal form at a rubber-meets-the-road level. The law of *proximity* means that in a random bunch of dots, dots grouped more closely together form a unit in our minds. The law of *similarity* means that if there's any variation in color in the larger group, we'll group together dots of similar color. The law of *symmetry* is self-explanatory; it means we'll favor

17

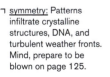

any organization of objects that tidies up the scene via symmetry. *Closure* refers to the mind's tendency to fill in a jagged line if it would make a complete form. *Continuity* fills in the complete object even if its form is obscured: A long rectangle is still a complete thing, even when partially hidden behind a tetrahedron. The dramatically named law of *common fate* groups dots moving in sync into a single unit. *Past experience* means we take context into consideration when evaluating the forms we see.

Gestaltists gave handy labels to other visual phenomena, too. *Emergence* describes how whole forms can seem to leap to the eye. We can puzzle slowly over what a blotchy curlicue, speckled dots, and a rounded triangle add up to. But if you're told to find the Dalmatian in that mess, suddenly and instantly that form will emerge for you. *Reification* refers to our tendency to add info to a visual stimulus, if that info completes the appearance of a form. *Multistability* refers to those optical illusions that force you to see two different forms in the same stimulus. (Blink: it's a rabbit's head. Blink again: it's a duck.) Finally, *invariance* describes how we recognize two forms as identical, despite superficial differences in appearance. For instance, a two-handled widget might be rotated upside-down, ten times bigger than its cousin-widget, or drawn sketchily while the cousin appears pixelated. None of this matters: two-handled widgets are fundamentally the same object.

Pattern designers rely on the laws of Gestalt to create certain effects. And sometimes they actively work against those effects. For instance, camouflage thwarts the laws of Gestalt in order to hide soldiers, military equipment, whole factories and cities from enemy eyes. Gestalt describes how we see objects, but also how we can manipulate patterns to render objects invisible.

Pattern Recognition: Now in Live 3-D Motion!

The Gestaltists nailed the *description* of our conscious perceptions of form and pattern. It remained for future generations of psychologists to *explain* them. They've begun by determining the stages in visual processing that culminate in certain visual perceptions, while harnessing whatever brain-imaging technologies can tell them about those processes.

Today psychologists think patterns help us with the business of *object segmentation*, or distinguishing one object from another nearby. Much recent progress has focused on 3-D object perception and object perception in motion. As it turns out, our neurons are remarkably attuned to different *depth-planes*. If two objects are 29 centimeters away and 30 centimeters away from us, respectively, that slight difference is represented by different patterns of neural activation in the visual cortex. Other things being equal, we're prone to interpret objects on the same depth-plane as a complete form, and to call that form a discrete pattern. Similarly, *object structure in motion* refers to how the brain "reads" patterns in motion to intuit a complete form. Imagine a perfectly clear drinking glass, slowly spinning in space:

● find the Dalmatian: For more lore on spotted-animal friends, turn to page 30.

☙ camouflage: Military efforts at tricking enemy eyes became increasingly theatrical over time. For papier-mâché heads and fake tree stumps, turn to page 112.

invisible, right? But say it's covered in white dot stickers whose motion we can watch. The moving pattern those dots make will cause our brains to backfill the cylindrical shape of the glass, an object we couldn't otherwise see.

Other psychologists have substantiated with Science a phenomenon illustrators have grasped intuitively for years: You can use a static pattern to suggest movement to the brain. A radial-starburst pattern, for instance, mimics the optic flow blur the retina experiences as you move forward in the world, like a ship going warp speed on *Star Trek*. Horizontal stripes, even when static, suggest moving sideways. Comic-book heroes punching bad guys have dynamic stripes around their fists for this very reason.

Pareidolia and Apophenia

The next time you swear you see repeating pandas in your bathroom floor tile, reach for these buzzwords to make you feel less crazy. *Pareidolia* describes the phenomenon of seeing imaginary forms—especially faces—in random stimuli. Pareidolia explains all kinds of magical thinking, from Rorschach tests, to "the man on the moon," to the uncanny way electrical sockets resemble faces, to seeing the Virgin Mary's face burned into a grilled-cheese sandwich. Pareidolia is also an auditory phenomenon: for instance, the way Beatles conspiracy-theorists hear the words "I buried Paul" murmured at the end of the song "Strawberry Fields Forever."

A cousin of pareidolia, *apophenia* refers to perceiving patterns where none exist. Those patterns might be visual, but quite often are just conceptual—for instance, the "gambler's fallacy" that hot streaks are actually a thing, despite all laws of statistics.

19

● Comic-book heroes punching bad guys: For a villain putting a sinister spin on a usually demure pattern, see Mister Polka-Dot on page 32.

✓ "gambler's fallacy": What do tigers have to do with gambling? Find out on page 56.

Dots

&

Spots

"Soundless as dots—on a disc of snow"
—from "Safe in their Alabaster Chambers …"
by Emily Dickinson

Do You Polka Dot?

The Polka Craze

Why do we call this iconic pattern "polka dots," anyhow? It's hardly a universal term. Germans, for one, often call it *Thalertupfen*, the coin-sized dots being named for *Thaler*, the currency of German-speaking Europe until the late 1800s and the term from which the English word *dollar* descends. Spaniards call polka dots *lunares*, or "little moons," while the

French describe something polka-dotted as *à pois*, "marked with peas."

In a win for the obvious, "polka dots" does, actually, stem from an extended craze for polka music that swept Europe from the 1830s through the 1860s. Legend has it a Hungarian dancing professor named Neruda discovered a peasant half-step dance in Bohemia that made everyone's toes feel a tad lighter. He called the dance "polka," reminiscent of the Czech words *pulka* ("little step") and *pole* ("field"). (*Polka* also means "Polish woman" in that language, the female counterpart of *Polák*.) Polka ripped through the Bohemian fields to Prague and Vienna, inflamed the ladies of Paris in 1840, hopped the Channel to engulf London in 1844, then set America ablaze. (James Polk enjoyed an accidental glow of popularity during his successful presidential bid that same year.) In 1845, the governor-general of Calcutta hosted a polka ball in honor of Queen Victoria: Polkamania Goes Global.

Polka's popularity was eye-popping. The London *Times*'s Paris correspondent during the period remarked: "Politics is for the moment suspended in public regard by the new and all-absorbing pursuit, the Polka." In 1844, the year polka arrived in London, *Punch* lampooned the incessant chatter about the dance in society circles: " 'Can you dance the Polka? Do you like the Polka? Polka—Polka—Polka—Polka'—it is enough to drive me mad." That same year, the Brighton *Gazette* tells an anecdote about a fashionable lady hassling the famed polka dance-master Perrot for private lessons. Not wishing to offend the influential dame by refusing outright, Perrot named his price as five pounds per lesson, "thinking that she would never dream of paying so enormous a sum; in that he was disappointed. 'The price is nothing,' said the lady. 'Give me the lesson.' Perrot did so; and in less than a week he had a great number of pupils at the same rate."

Sheet-music composers cranked out polkas in extraordinary variety: the "Aurora Borealis Polka," the "Happy Family Polka," the "General Grant Polka," "Hiawatha's Bridal Polka," "Pussy's Polka" (subtitle: "Composed by Kitty"), the "Katy-did Polka," the "Thunder and Lightning Polka," "Barnum's Baby Show Polka." Every occasion, every clique, every weather pattern, every passing mood was stamped with its own perfect polka.

Fevers want catching. Marketers during this period hawked every product they could as polka-themed—including foods like polka pudding (a boozy confection of orange-water-flavored cream, drizzled with sherry "polka sauce"). But much of it—polka curtains, polka hats—was identifiable by the spattering of sprightly dots. The connection between the dance and the pattern on all that spotted merch is murky at best. Possibly the spotted pattern evoked the lively half-step of the dance. It's also unclear whether marketers intended all those polka hats, vests, and shoes as dancewear, or if calling something "polka" just made a product seem more cheerful. In any event, most sources credit *Godey's Lady's Book*—the *Good Housekeeping* of its day—as naming the pattern "polka dot." The polka-product craze—and the dance craze itself—eventually flamed out, but the name "polka dots" for the pattern stuck.

Who Owns Polka Dots?

Long after society had ceased its toe-tapping, polka dots persisted, and by 1936, the pattern was still sufficiently big business that it featured prominently in debate of the so-called Duffy bill, a broad-scale revision of U.S. copyright law. The Vandenberg amendment to this bill provided "for copyright in designs for articles of manufacture heretofore protected by patent." It was, in other words, something of a legal-wonk quibble, not expected to generate any splashy newspaper headlines. Shoe designer Mary Bendalari argued for the copyright provision in front of the House Patents Committee against Irving Fox of the National Retail Dry

Goods Association, who represented the con side. The question: Should customized versions of polka-dot and daisy patterns, strap-sandal designs (by Miss Bendalari and others), domestic furniture designs, and dress-making patterns in magazines be protected for their creators under copyright law, patent law, or any law at all? The hearing stands apart for its high-toned, dinner-theater quality.

Though Miss Bendalari did not wear polka dots for her appearance in front of the committee, she did wear an original design she called the "Constitutional Inspiration": a dark-blue-and-white striped chiffon dress with a belt decoration of red and blue stars, topped with a corsage cluster of small gold stars. When Irving Fox challenged how one would copyright a polka dot or any arrangement thereof, Bendalari spunkily (if somewhat vaguely) retorted, "There is only one principle here, no matter how you smother it with polka dots . . . We base our demand for copyright protection on the Constitution, in which our right to it is specifically provided." Meanwhile, manufacturers of macho industrial designs like automobile products and accessories had asked for exemption from the amendment, an exception Mr. Fox cited as proof the proposal was "bad law for any industry." (That's one interpretation. It could also mean auto manufacturers preferred protection under patent law versus copyright law, or that they wished to preserve the right to copycat each other freely.)

In the end, the Vandenberg amendment was scrapped for vagueness and un-enforceability. Bendalari may've lost her cause, but her plucky defense (and fetchingly patriotic

ensemble) boosted the polka dot as the energetic *motif nouveau* for modern women.

Polka Dots, Moonbeams, and Patriotism

Polka dots enjoyed a resurgence—one particularly female yet oddly ambiguous—in early twentieth-century America. Clean and simple in its machine-printed version, the pattern exuded a lively wholesomeness appropriate for children and popular on bedsheets, bassinets, and nightgowns. And yet it was recognized that the tiniest of tweaks—packing the dots tightly together, say, or letting them jostle and overlap—could produce an exhilarating disorientation. Together, these associations fed the feminine aura of the polka dot—sweet innocence and heady sexiness rolled into one.

The year 1940 marked the polka dot's second heyday in ladies' fashion: It enjoyed a popularity not seen since its inception. "You can sign your fashion life away on the polka-dotted line, and you'll never regret it this season," the *Los Angeles Times* remarked in spring 1940. That was also the year of Frank Sinatra's first breakout hit, a romantic ditty called "Polka Dots and Moonbeams." Three years later, the *Washington Post* dubbed polka dots *the* pattern of American democratic values: "What we mean by a print with social significance is one that most people can wear most of the time. The whole family of polka dots falls into that category even if they don't <u>spell 'Remember Pearl Harbor' in code</u>. The full-grown variety in particular makes a clean-cut

25

/ <u>spell 'Remember Pearl</u>
¬ <u>Harbor' in code:</u> Patterns
☙ and motifs have been jumbled into fresh alphabets to encode all kinds of information. To parse the stripes in bar codes, see page 62.

¬ For all the different things a series of knots can mean, see page 122.

☙ For three ways to "say it with flowers"—according to traditional textiles in Madagascar, Turkey, and Kenya—see page 107.

I brake
for birds.

I have touched
glitter in the last
twenty-four hours.

I spend my entire day
talking to children.

I rock *a lot* of polka dots.

And I find it fundamentally strange that you're not a dessert person.

—Zooey Deschanel

as Jess in the TV show *New Girl*

monotone pattern that is neither dizzy nor monotonous. It is as good in a close-up as it is in perspective and manages to be in pleasing proportion to all kinds of figures. It requires no more than a casual acquaintance with the cleaner." Upbeat, wholesome, versatile, and practical, polka dots were the almost-official pattern of the patriotic home front.

The Girl in the Polka-Dotted Dress

A fringe of suspicious characters ringed Robert F. Kennedy's 1968 assassination, including a possibly shifty security guard (exonerated), a *Manchurian Candidate*–style brainwasher (wholly imagined), and one girl wearing a polka-dotted dress (partially imagined). Misgivings attached to the girl when she reportedly burst through the crowd accompanied by a man, shouting, "We shot him! We shot him!" A Kennedy volunteer claimed the girl confirmed that by "him" she meant Kennedy. Other eyewitnesses recalled seeing the girl with the shooter Sirhan B. Sirhan in, among other locales, the kitchen where the assassination took place. When the girl—nineteen-year-old Kathy Fulmer of Los Angeles—came forward for further questioning, the media paid surprisingly close attention to her outfits: to the shooting, Fulmer wore a blonde wig over her brown hair, and a solid green suit offset by a polka-dotted scarf. She wore the same wig with a "bright lavender" dress for questioning. In popular imagination, the dots on the girl's

scarf swelled over her bright dress, too. But Ms. Fulmer's supposed murderous streak faded upon closer examination: she was guilty only of very eye-catching accessorizing.

Polka-Dot Bikini

That devastating beach costume, the bikini, is most iconic when sprinkled with cheerful polka dots. Possibly the first depiction of a bikini dates to 5600 B.C.E., in which the mother-goddess of the Turkish city of Çatalhöyük sits astride two leopards in a kicky two-piece costume. Ancient Roman ladies regularly bound their breasts (with matching shorts), a form of practical undergarment that could also be worn for swimming or bathing. In addition to providing support, Ovid thought, the breast-band was a perfect hiding place for love letters.

The modern bikini appeared in 1913—though it didn't yet have its name. Sportswear designer Carl Jantzen's two-piece hugged the figure but covered a lot of skin; it was intended as a pragmatic design, marking the arrival of women's swimming as an official Olympic event. But Jantzen's athletic and patriotic justification cut no ice with the bikini's prudish detractors: cue blue-balled howling by parsons and their ilk.

Bikinis continued their gradual miniaturization in 1946, when two French designers simultaneously introduced two new two-pieces. Jacques Heim's "*l'Atome*" revealed a slice of belly while keeping the navel covered; Louis Réard's "bikini" plunged farther south and was made of a scant thirty inches

supposed murderous streak: The striped Beast of Gévaudan terrorized the French countryside from 1764 to 1767, eating mothers and babies and generally causing a Bigfoot-style ruckus. To revisit a pre-Revolutionary tabloid sensation, see page 57.

blue-balled howling by parsons: For the yowling of Carmelite monks at Pope Boniface VIII in 1287, see page 47.

of fabric. It was named after the Bikini Atoll atomic test site in the Pacific Ocean; with his design Réard claimed to have "split *l'Atome*"—and he hired a (normally) nude showgirl to model it. Eagerly anticipating a publicity scandal, he printed the bikini's backside to simulate newsprint and watched the media outrage—and sales—roll in. The newsprint pattern on bikinis didn't stick around long. These days the polka dot is more prevalent—indeed, it's become iconic. But it might still owe something to Réard. One imagines polka dots and bikinis got so intertwined because the bikini's history suggests its destiny lies in dwindling down to three tiny, anatomically spaced dots.

Of course, the association between dots and bikinis was cemented by Brian Hyland's 1960 song, "Itsy Bitsy Teeny Weeny Yellow Polka Dot Bikini." The song hit #1 on the Billboard Hot 100 in August 1960 and spawned numerous remakes in languages around the globe. In 1961 filmmaker Billy Wilder distorted that song into a torture device in a pivotal scene in his film *One, Two, Three*. An American Coca-Cola executive in recently walled-off West Berlin welcomes his boss's daughter to town, where she promptly and calamitously marries an East German Communist zealot. With a surprise visit from the boss looming, the Coke exec wastes no time in branding the young lover as a Yankee spy and siccing the Stasi on him. They wear down his resistance with screechy, repeated record-playing of Hyland's hit. Here the connection between the transgressive bikini and polka dots becomes more sinister: the Communist's off-bounds romance disrupted by relentless capitalist jingles, those dots boring into the skull.

Menace

A Dreaded Spot

The innocent, bouncing polka dot is rooted in earthier stuff. Medieval Europeans rarely wore dotted patterns on fabric, because it was virtually impossible to space the dots evenly without the help of machines. In an era of iffy medicine, irregularly spaced dots made people think of outbreaks of incurable diseases like leprosy, syphilis, smallpox, bubonic plague, and measles. Steven Connor, professor of English and cultural historian at the University of Cambridge, explains: "Irregularly spotted fabrics are ominous not just because they are reminiscent of blemishes on the skin, but also because they are uncomfortable reminders of the ominous markings of other fabrics: the blood in the handkerchief that was a traditional sign of tuberculosis, and the 'spotting' . . . which may presage a miscarriage in early pregnancy. Desdemona's strawberry-spotted handkerchief, which leads to such disasters in *Othello*, joins together the associations of disease, <u>deception</u>, lust and corruption."

Ironically, spottedness was most reviled at its onset: One or two spots was judged much more unclean than a uniformly spotted surface. Leviticus 13: 12–13 explains that a priest presented with an early-stage leper must pronounce him unclean, particularly when "the appearance of the plague be deeper than the skin of his flesh." However, if "the leprosy cover all the skin of him that hath the plague from his head even to his feet . . . [the priest] shall pronounce him clean that hath the plague: it is all turned white: he is clean." In other words, a full-blown case of leprosy signified a person on the threshold of death, someone whose suffering on earth might soon shade into a spotless transcendence to heaven. A single glaring spot, on the other hand, suggested an incomplete (and therefore unnerving) transformation, one with potential to spread dangerously in all directions.

The Panther and His Spots

In both mythology and modern taxonomy, "panther" (genus *Panthera*) is an umbrella term for large, spotted feral cats: specifically, the leopard in Africa and Asia, the cougar or mountain lion in North America, and the jaguar in South and Central America. Pre-modern Europeans considered the panther symbolic of Christ, but with slightly more ghoulish manners. In his seventh-century bestiary *Etymologies*, Isidore of Seville writes: "The panther (*pantera*) takes its name from the Greek word for 'all' (*pan*), because the panther is the friend of all beasts other than the dragon. They are covered with black and white circles that look like eyes. Female panthers can only give birth once, because the cubs, in their eagerness to escape the womb, tear at their mother with their claws so she can no longer conceive." Later, thirteenth-century writer Bartholomaeus Angelicus described a medieval belief about the panther's sleeping habits. After

🐾 <u>deception:</u> The history of camouflage starts with the newfound need in World War I to hide war matériel from enemy airplanes. It ends with inflatable tanks, decoy heads, magicians in colonel stripes, jazzy warships, and other hijinks. See page 111.

feasting on a big kill, the panther supposedly retreats into a cave for three days of slumber, à la Christ before his resurrection. Yawning himself awake, the panther's sweet-smelling breath is said to lure his next meal straight to him—a distinctly more predatory form of evangelism than Jesus suffering little children to come unto him. Only the devil's avatar, the dragon, could resist the panther's sacred perfume.

Not all cultures see the panther as the ultimate Good Guy. The Uyghur people substitute a spotted leopard for the wolf in their version of Little Red Riding Hood. Here's how their folk tale goes: A mother packs up her son for a visit to the grandmother, leaving her two daughters home alone. En route, the mother meets a friendly leopard, who offers to brush her hair while she stops to rest. Predictably, the mother's trust proves misplaced when the leopard starts to snack on the mother's skin, then makes an entire meal of both mother and son. Dressing in the mother's clothes, the leopard stuffs the boy's still-meaty bones into the mother's basket and heads back to the family homestead, where he bluffs his way through the daughters' suspicious questioning and gains entry. (When confronted with the what-big-spots-you-have challenge, the leopard explains that Grandmother had no guest bed, so he had to sleep on a sack of peas, which left dot-like impressions on his face.)

Later, when the daughters are tucked into bed, the leopard cracks open his basket and continues his feast on the son's meaty bones. The daughters awaken, ask for a taste of the "beets" the leopard is eating, recognize their brother's finger among the morsels, and promptly freak out.

Outed, the leopard attacks. The girls narrowly escape and, momentarily discouraged, the leopard bolts off.

The next morning, the daughters sit tearfully on their stoop. How to survive the leopard's inevitable return? Sympathetic passersby listen to their plight, then place unexplained gifts in strategic points around the girls' house: a pillow festooned with <u>needles</u> sharp side out; a scorpion; an egg; a tortoise; and two wooden cudgels.

Uyghur Folk-Lore and Legend connects all these gifts in a revenge-finale poised between Rube Goldberg machine and Wile E. Coyote:

> When it became evening, the leopard came to their house. He sat down on the chair . . . but the needles in the cushion stabbed him. Then he went into the kitchen to make a fire in order to see what had stabbed him, but his hand got stung by the scorpion. And when he had finally lighted the fire, the egg burst and . . . blinded one of his eyes. Then he walked into the yard and put his hand into the water jar to cool it down. Then the tortoise bit off his hand. In great pain he ran out of the gate door into the street, when the wooden cudgels fell down on his head and beat him to death.

B <u>needles:</u> For a super-compressed lesson in textile history, see page 11.

Mister Polka-Dot

In 1962, the Gotham City of *Batman* comic books was plagued by one Abner Krill, who, for reasons unknown, donned a polka-dotted costume and initiated an extended crime spree. Mister Polka-Dot resembled a well-muscled <u>gumball machine</u> in his getup, which married form *and* function. By manipulating his special controller belt, he could cause the flat polka dots on his suit to swell alarmingly, then transform themselves into tools handy for criminal mayhem. Of particular usefulness was his Flying Polka Dot, a roly-poly getaway vehicle.

What exactly his dottedness conveyed to midcentury comic readers is an open question: Television pixels? Polio germs? Radioactive ions? Secret Communist leanings? Cold War America was rife with invisible dots, ambivalent spores infiltrating society for good or ill.

Charms & Signals

Healing Dots

Bushmen rock art in southern Africa buzzes with three kinds of dots: "microdots," "finger dots," and "finger flecks." All depict supernatural potency at different stages.

To make their dot-heavy art, Bushmen healers induce a spirit trance—basically, get high—and then record their shamanistic visions in rock painting. First they cut their scalps and squeeze the juice from an <u>onion-like bulb</u> called *kwashi* into the wounds. This introduces the plant's <u>hallucinogens</u> directly into their bloodstreams. The first signs the drugs are kicking in are painful sensations radiating up and down the spine and a vise-like pressure on the stomach and innards. The healers call this feeling *num*, the sacred healing energy, and depict its sensation in their paintings with microdots.

Next comes the finger-dot phase. Slightly larger than microdots, finger dots spiral around objects, animals, and scenes that the healers consider supernaturally charged up and ready for action. Like hippies gazing at psychedelic posters to intensify their high, healers contemplate old paintings to deepen their trance enough to make a new one.

Last on the scene are the elongated blobs called finger flecks. Like the agitated lines and BLAMMO! starbursts of Western comic books, finger flecks depict motion, activity, hubbub—magic now unleashed and circulating. (The hubbub depicted by finger-fleck dots might consist of other, active rituals: dancing, clashes between healers and spirit animals, or fights.)

The purpose of spirit trances is tangled up with its

⟋ <u>gumball machine:</u> Speaking of confections, how did candy canes get their stripes? See page 69.

☙ <u>onion-like bulb:</u> Bulbous paisley has been variously likened to a lotus, cypress, or mango (in the fruit-and-veg category) as well as to leeches and dragons (in the animal category). For more, see page 95. Similarly, fleur-de-lis is said to have sprung from irises, lotuses, and doves. See page 103.

B <u>hallucinogens:</u> Optical illusions reveal kinks in how our brains process patterns. For a speed course in pattern cognition, see page 17.

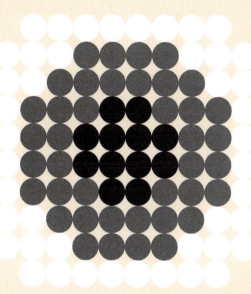

I discovered about 150 dots is the minimum number of dots to make a specific recognizable person. You can make something that looks like a head, with fewer dots, but you won't be able to give much information about who it is.

—Artist Chuck Close, who specializes in painting large-scale portraits in pixelated dots dottiness, too. The ritual's aim is to "pull sickness" out of a sufferer, a struggle the uncertain odds of which depend on the strength of the sickness's dots, and on the surge of dots healers can muster in response.

Dots Make the Man

Both the Banda tribe of the Central African Republic and the Lega people of the Democratic Republic of Congo traditionally daub adolescent boys with white dots for male-initiation rites. The Lega rite is particularly dot-obsessed: It calls for the young man, adorned in dots, to knock incessantly at a specially constructed polka-dotted door (*keibi*) as a test of his piety and persistence. Eventually he's admitted and presents gifts to his father in thanks. All the participants, their skins also speckled with white dots, pay homage to the *keibi*, whose dots represent the leopard, a beast that frightens goats and other animals but doesn't faze the young hunter. The initiation ends in a group dance, where the adult "herd of elephants" (*idumbu*) welcomes the "little elephant" (*kalupepe*), together making a whirling, energetic blur of dots.

Japanese *Ensō*

Clear-eyed, caffeine-free, with mind and bowels emptied, dip a sable brush into black ink and—whoosh!—draw a perfect circle, or *ensō*. "The *ensō* is perhaps the most

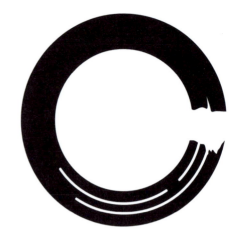

common subject of Zen calligraphy," writes John Daido Loori, abbot of the Zen Mountain Monastery in the Catskills in upstate New York and author of several books on Zen. "It symbolizes enlightenment, power, and the universe itself . . . It is believed that the character of the artist is fully exposed in how he or she draws an *ensō*. Only a person who is mentally and spiritually complete can draw a true one. Some artists practice drawing an *ensō* daily as a spiritual exercise." If practiced daily, *ensō*–making will fill trashcans with sheets and sheets of handmade, de facto polka dots.

Each *ensō* consists of the circle itself, flanked by a quotation or comment, and finished with the calligrapher's *hanko*, or name stamp. It's the juxtaposition of text and circle that makes an *ensō* particularly evocative. Often calligraphers leave *ensō* unclosed or irregular, an homage to the Japanese ideal of *fukinsei* (不均斉), asymmetry or the denial of perfection.

Ensō can also be tongue-in-cheek. A famous triangular *ensō* by Keido Fukushima comes with the inscription, "Even this is a circle." And sometimes *ensō*-makers do appreciate the mind-clearing pleasures of a snack break. Japanese office snacks like dumplings and rice or sesame cakes, downed with copious cups of tea, march through *ensō* parables. When one is spied by one's boss in the break room for the umpteenth time, present her with a freshly microwaved cookie while repeating the words of eighteenth-century calligrapher Setsudō's "Baking Pan": "Like a baking pan/worldly passions/are engulfed in fire." That long-overdue TPS report will wither in significance.

Often calligraphers fill their *ensō* with depictions of the Zen ox-herding parable. A story in ten discrete moments, this parable from eleventh-century China compares the path to enlightenment to a herding boy's search for his missing ox. After initial fumbling, the boy nabs the ox by stage five (*Tokugyuu*), killing the dramatic tension of the A-plot while launching a more compelling B-plot: What does all this ox-herding mean, anyhow? By stage eight (*Ningyuu guboo*), both the self and the ox are forgotten, a realization usually depicted as an all-obliterating *ensō*. By the tenth and final stage, the enlightened ox-herd and his blissed-out animal head back into city life to spread Zen to others.

At least one tough job interview has been aced thanks to a well-executed *ensō*. When Pope Benedict XI invited Giotto to a tryout to paint the fresco on an entranceway of Old Saint Peter's Basilica in the Vatican, Giotto immediately dashed out a perfect circle in red ink and handed it back to the (startled) courier. The courier asked if this was the only work sample he intended to offer, to which Giotto coolly replied: "It is both enough and too much." Clearly a pope more receptive to chutzpah than most, Benedict agreed and gave him the job.

The Quixotic Quincunx

Roll a die and hit five, and you will be peering down at a quincunx, a motif consisting of five dots staggered on the diagonal. Quincunx—or, if you prefer a less skunky-sounding appellation, *quinconce* in French—first sprang into existence on Roman coins. A brass quincunx was worth five twelfths of a unit of currency called the *as*. Medieval heraldry renamed this motif *in saltire*, a way of tidily organizing five charges (or visual elements) in a family crest. (Sadly, their term for the motif of dots only caught on in heraldry-buff circles.) Quincunx later proved a handy organizing device for architects, orchard planters, tile workers, or anyone tasked with herding a teeming multiplicity into an orderly grid.

Quincunxes even brought a reassuring orderliness to mathematics. The nineteenth-century British mathematician Sir Francis Galton invented a machine—known as "the Galton box," the "bean machine," or simply "the quincunx"—to demonstrate a principle of probability

---

⟋ Pope Benedict XI: A fussier Pope B. outlawed striped clothing for monks in the thirteenth century, riling up the Carmelites in their brown-and-white-striped habits. See page 47.

⟋ medieval heraldry: See page 48 for heraldry Euro-style.

■ architects: To learn bricklayer's lingo for the six different sides of a brick, from "shiner" to "sailor," see page 90.

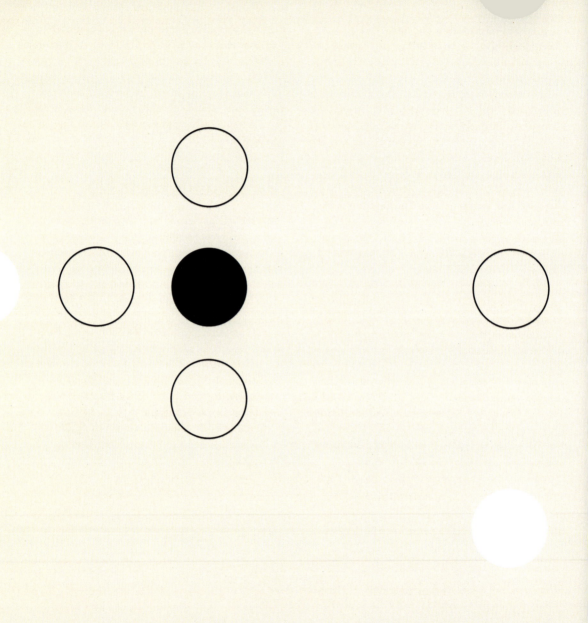

called normal distribution. It consists of a vertical board interleaved with pins staggered in a quincunx pattern. When you drop balls into the maze from the top, they <u>zig and zag</u> until landing in the one-ball-wide gutter at the bottom. Along their way they take any number of paths, but if the machine is sufficiently wide they stack into a shape resembling a bell curve, normally distributed: voilà!

Quincunx reveals its seamier side in the realm of <u>tattoos</u>. Prisoners have been known to tattoo a quincunx onto the tender web of flesh between index finger and thumb; what it means depends on the prisoner's affiliations. To the Portuguese, it signifies the five oozing wounds of Christ; to Vietnamese gang members, it reminds them of the five golden T's: *Tình, Tiền, Tù, Tội, Thù* (love, money, prison, crime, revenge). For gents locked up in the United Kingdom, the five dots sum up their winning dating philosophy: "Find Her, Follow Her, Finger Her, Fuck Her, Forget Her." Across many cultures—from South America to Russia and Armenia—the four outer dots swarm the fifth in the center, like policemen and guards surrounding the <u>prisoner</u>, soon to be replaced by prison walls.

The unlikely granddaddy of quincunx tattoos is Thomas Edison. Edison invented the electric pen in 1875, thinking its speed—fifty punctures per second—could make a rapid stencil copy of an image or text. You'd then pass an inked roller over the stencil to make multiple copies on paper. Why one might turn to such a device when the printing press was already three centuries deep into its success was a question that occurred to many of the electric pen's would-be users. Unsurprisingly, it proved a massive flop.

Yet the electric pen staged a <u>phoenix-like comeback</u> when tattooists stumbled on it. In 1891, a New York tattoo artist named Samuel F. O'Reilly produced an electric tattoo needle based on Edison's pen, making tattooing both faster and more precise. An inveterate showman, Edison celebrated the pen's accidental success by inking a quincunx with the pen onto his left forearm.

Five Adinkra Dots

It's fun to "read" and misread the same pattern through different cultural goggles. What the French call the *quinconce* pattern, the Asante people of Ghana would see as one of several symbols on adinkra cloth, traditionally worn to funerals but now brightly saturated with color for any special occasion. To make adinkra, you print fine cloth with thick black dye in a grid. Then using calabashes carved with various symbols, you stamp the cloth and fill the grid in. The resulting adinkra is a gloriously detailed fabric, dense with meaning. It's formalwear that would be ideally accessorized with its own decoder ring—or, less elegantly, a telephone-book-sized guide to the ever-proliferating alphabet of adinkra symbols.

If the five dots just touch each other in a dice-style X, that's called *mpuannum*, or "five tufts of hair." This represents the priestly office and its hallmarks of loyalty and adroitness. But if the dots crowd each other and overlap slightly, that's a different motif: *kintinkantan*, or "puffed up extravagance."

⟋ **zig and zag:** See page 68.

● **tattoos:** When the femme-Nikita character in Alexandre Dumas's novel *The Three Musketeers* flashes her fleur-de-lis tattoo, it signals that she's not just a sexy nemesis but a former felon. On the practice of *fleurdeliser*, see page 105.

⟋ **prisoner:** Why did prisoners wear black-and-white-striped uniforms for so long? See page 48.

■ **phoenix-like comeback:** Never did a pattern induce Elvis-like swooning or country-music-level nostalgia as did tartan (aka plaid) after the British banned it in 1746. See page 73.

DICE, N.

SMALL POLKA-DOTTED CUBES

OF IVORY, CONSTRUCTED

LIKE A LAWYER TO LIE

ON ANY SIDE, BUT COMMONLY

ON THE WRONG ONE.

—from *The Devil's Dictionary* by
Ambrose Gwinnett Bierce

**On her left breast
A mole cinque-spotted,
like the crimson drops
I' th' bottom of a cowslip.**

—from Shakespeare's *Cymbeline* (Act 2,
Scene 2, lines 37–39), when Iachimo
watches Imogen sleeping

A cousin of these two symbols is *mate masie*, four ovals arranged in a tight square. Each oval includes a dark inner shape that makes these look like Kilroy cartoon eyes—or more accurately ears, as *mate masie* means "what I hear, I keep." *Mate masie* evokes knowledge, wisdom, and prudence. If those pupils travel heavenward and thin into tiny vertical slits, that's considered yet another adinkra motif: *me ware wo*, "I shall marry you." It conveys commitment and perseverance—and, parenthetically, resembles the eye-rolling necessary to ignore a spouse's more grating habits.

Patching and Mole Reading

From the 1590s until the 1720s, European ladies engaged in a protracted craze for "patching," the practice of sticking dots of black fabric to the face—a dot often being called a *moucheron*, French for "little fly." Moucherons could either cover a blemish or simply offset, and therefore enhance, the beauty of otherwise flawless skin.

Patches sometimes imitated real moles, gaming a concurrent fashion of "reading" the position of moles on one's body to tell the moled-one's fortune. For instance, a lady might slap a moucheron on her right shoulder, a position that signaled to suitors that married life with her "betokeneth much outward happiness; she will be fruitful, honorable, in goods and chattel abounding." Europeans weren't alone in this style of mole-interpretation; the Chinese and Japanese also anxiously consulted their skin for hints about their destinies. "Moles are diagnostic characters," Japanese peasants told folklorist Gwladys Hughes Simon when she was gathering superstitions and home remedies in post–World War II Japan. "Near the mouth, they show you are greedy in eating; near the eye, you are a blubberer; between the eyes, you are a wise man." Europeans would read those same moles differently: The lip-mole, for instance, promised "exceeding good fortune" on a man, but debauchery on a woman. Moreover, exact position mattered. According to *The Book of Skin* by historian Steven Connor, European fortune-tellers thought "a mole on the left side of the mouth denotes vanity and pride, and unlawful offspring to provide for." (The Chinese would interpret this same mole as "tending to have foot problems; need to prevent water-related accidents.")

Ever primed for outrage at popular fads, the Puritans happily took aim at patching. In the 1630 poem "The Vicious Courtier," Nathaniel Richards rails against female vanity made manifest in patches:

> Why Oyles? Waters for Teeth? Why
> void of Grace?
> With spots (like Rat-Dung) to blacke-
> patch the face? . . .
> Why wrong Heav'ns workmanship,
> with such hie sin? . . .
> The painted outside of a tempting Face,
> Spotted with Hell, stands sequestred
> from Grace.

/ unlawful offspring: A "bar sinister," or left-leaning diagonal stripe, marks bastard family lines in medieval European heraldry; see page 49.

☙ popular fads: Camouflage's practical popularity during wartime dribbled over after World War II into civilian life, from camo-themed amusement parks and board games to slenderizing fashion tricks; see page 115. For paisley's precipitous rise and fall in popularity, see page 97; for same of plaid, see page 76.

/ Rat-Dung: The 1920s manifesto *The Structure of Iki* details what's "hot or not" according to Japanese aesthetics. Extremely *iki* colors run distinctly counter to Western ideas of attractiveness; they especially dug mouse-brown and rat-gray. See page 63.

A patch-addicted lady—a relative of seventeenth-century scientist Kenneth Digby—never showed herself in public without a multitude of patches shaped like stars or crescents on her face and neck. When she became pregnant, Digby warned her to drop her patching fixation, lest sympathetic vibes between the vain mother and unborn baby similarly "mark" the child. Alarmed, she abandoned the practice, but the child was indeed born with a dark blotch on its forehead. (So persistent was this belief that a mother's feelings of alarm or yearning could stamp a child in utero that birthmarks became known as "longing marks." The idea lingers in the modern French word for birthmarks, *envies*.)

A plague outbreak in London in 1665 detracted somewhat from patching's allure, dots once again uncomfortably evoking skin disease and its nasty causes, like <u>prostitution</u>. Yet the practice persisted for another fifty years.

Dot Art & Activism

"Burn Wall Street. Wall Street men must become farmers and fishermen . . . OBLITERATE THE MEN OF WALL STREET WITH POLKA DOTS ON THEIR NAKED BODIES. BE IN . . . BE NAKED, NAKED, NAKED," wrote artist Yayoi Kusama in a 1968 manifesto-qua-press-release announcing her performance series *The Anatomic Explosion*. Art critic Andrew Solomon described the dot-addled scene in *Artforum* (1997): "Across from the New York Stock Exchange on Wall Street, four nude dancers gyrated to the rhythm of bongo drummers, while Kusama, accompanied by her lawyer, spray painted blue polka dots on their naked bodies." (One presumes the nonplussed lawyer on Kusama's <u>payroll</u> felt exempt from her critiques of capitalist power-mongers.)

Covering her artwork with them since the 1960s, Kusama considers dots to be an expression of cosmic pixilation, an almost vicious democracy in which every object, person, and atmospheric vibe boils down to the particulate. "Our earth is only one polka dot among millions of others," she explained. "When Kusama paints your body with polka dots you become part of the <u>unity of the universe</u>." Elaborating in a more—yes—dotty vein, Kusama proffered President-elect Richard Nixon some advice in a public 1968 letter: "You can't eradicate violence by using more violence. This truth is written in the spheres with which I will lovingly, soothingly adorn your hard, masculine body. Gently! Gently! dear Richard. Calm your manly fighting spirit!"

By 2006, having committed herself to a mental institution thirty years earlier (and modified her <u>anti-capitalist stance</u> to the point of designing mobile phone covers, T-shirts, and other dotted tchotchkes), Kusama's love for dots softened in tone if not ardency. "[Dots] scatter proliferating love in the universe and raise my mind to the height of the sky," she writes. "This mysterious dots obsession."

42

⟋ prostitution: In medieval European painting, stripes designated social outcasts, from tax collectors to madmen to prostitutes. See page 47.

■ payroll: On the Indonesian island of Buton, villagers used a specific black-and-white checkered cloth as currency until the mid-twentieth century; see page 34.

⟋ unity of the universe: Korean saek-dong and Chinese lishui are two life-giving stripes that confer on the wearer cosmic good vibes. See page 54.

❤ anti-capitalist stance: Another notable figure in pattern history who dithered between capitalism and socialism was nineteenth-century English wallpaper designer William Morris. See page 94.

Even a small dot
can stop a big sentence

• • •

but a few more dots
can give a continuity.

—ANONYMOUS

Lines

Stripes

A LINE IS A DOT THAT

WENT FOR A WALK.

—PAUL KLEE

Work, Caste, & Out- casts

Stripe as Censor

Anyone who can't imagine monks squabbling over clothes has never had their hem measured by Catholic-school nuns. The trouble began in 1254 as Louis IX of France, later known as Saint Louis, returned from a failed crusade in the Holy Land, bringing with him a retinue of Carmelite monks sporting their habitual garb of brown-and-white-striped robes. *Sacrebleu!* Outraged sensation at the monks' clothing radiated up and down the streets of Paris, a reaction now more strictly confined to, say, wearing <u>ass-less chaps to Sunday school</u>.

Art historian Michel Pastoureau explains this odd reaction in his book *The Devil's Cloth: A History of Stripes*. To the medieval eye stripes marked "outcasts or reprobates, from the Jew and the heretic to the clown and the juggler, and including not only the leper, the hangman and the prostitute but also the disloyal knight of the Round Table, the madman of the Book of Psalms, and the character of Judas." While spots signaled disease (either physical or moral), wearing stripes designated people "barred" from polite society. Those Parisians scandalized by the Carmelites might have pointed to Leviticus 19:19: "You will not wear upon yourself a garment that is made of two." Whether that "two" meant "two different kinds of textile" or "two contrasting colors," i.e. stripes, seems open to debate by us moderns. But by the thirteenth century the bias against stripes was well entrenched in Europe's sumptuary laws, its literary conventions, and its artwork: Disreputable guys and slutty girls were helpfully depicted wearing stripes to signal their outsider status.

Pastoureau beams us into the <u>visual-processing brains</u> of medieval Europeans to see those stripes the way they did. Beyond the ambiguous biblical injunction, dots and stripes played havoc with the medieval preference for reading any visual image in layers, from the bottommost layer to the foreground. With stripes and dots, "such a reading is no longer possible," writes Pastoureau. "There is not a level

---

● <u>ass-less chaps to Sunday school:</u> Prudes and parsons alike got plenty exercised over another skimpy article of clothing, the polka-dotted bikini. See page 28.

B <u>visual-processing brains:</u> How do we perceive patterns cognitively—and why are they useful to notice at all? Page 17 provides the scoop.

below and a level above, a background color and a figure color . . . the structure *is* the figure. Is that where the scandal originates?"

Anti-stripes suspicion aside, respectable Frenchmen also sniffed at the Carmelites' explanation for their striped habit: It recalled their founder Elijah, who tossed his white cloak down to his brother while being dragged to heaven in a fiery chariot. The stripes were, in effect, holy skidmarks.

The matter of the Carmelite stripes grew so heated that Pope Boniface VIII was forced to intervene. In 1287— thirty-three years after the debate started—he banned striped clothing for all religious orders.

Striped Prison Uniforms

The medieval suspicion of stripes carried over to black-and-white-striped prisoners' uniforms, which first emerged in eighteenth-century penal colonies in the New World. The pattern's high visibility discouraged escape attempts while serving prisoners a daily dose of humiliation, like sartorial cod-liver oil. "The horizontal stripes of black and white, applied in such broad widths, appear vulgar and brash— something undignified imposed upon the wearer," write Mark Hampshire and Keith Stephenson in *Communicating with Pattern: Stripes*. The uniforms' horizontal stripes also echoed the thick vertical bars of the prison itself. Together, the interlocking black stripes visually canceled prisoners' bodies out.

Fittingly, many languages connect the word *stripes* to

ideas of imprisonment, deprivation, and punishment. The French word *rayer* means both "to stripe" and "to strike off a list," paralleling the English words *stripe* and *strip*. In Latin, words like *stria* (stripe or streak) and *striga* (row, line, or furrow) stem from the verb *stringere*, which encompasses ideas of clasping or depriving, and its close cousin *constringere*, to imprison.

Black-and-white prison stripes fell from favor in the latter twentieth century, evoking extreme abuses like chain gangs and Nazi concentration camp uniforms. While high-visibility-orange dominates prison uniforms in most states, at least one municipality has preserved stripes in a very outlandish style. According to a *Slate* Explainer column by Christopher Beam in 2010, "Cleveland County [in Oklahoma] makes prisoners wear pink shirts and yellow-and-white striped pants, which sheriff's officials say makes escape more difficult." How easily can escapees blend in while dressing like Easter eggs?

Medieval Heraldry

Heraldry is an underappreciated Rosetta Stone of Western patterning.

Originating in medieval Europe as a way to identify jousters at tournaments, heraldry is the study of coats of arms—also known as "heraldic devices" or "shields"—that have bedecked establishmentarian surfaces for a millennium: from university stationery to old-style brewery labels to the scrolled gatework that billionaires hide behind. A heraldic

---

- visually canceled prisoners' bodies out: Convicts the world over tattoo themselves with a five-dot arrangement known as a quincunx. For its many meanings, turn to page 38.

- imprison: Sporting a fleur-de-lis tattoo used to brand one as a French felon. For more on the practice of *fleurdeliser*, see page 105.

- high-visibility-orange: Also favored by hunters, when not sporting camouflage. For the unlikely history of this pattern, see page 109.

device identifies a family and its possessions, and how that device evolves over time reveals that family's history.

Still, its modern fans aren't a popular lot: titled English codgers. Renaissance-fair actors. Dungeons & Dragons players. Historians in un-ironic bow ties. <u>Brutal dictators searching for bona fides</u>. Social climbers.

And yet it's fun to learn the visual grammar of heraldry, a system of rules known as "blazon." It feels <u>faintly punk-rock</u> to parse a heraldic device knowledgeably, to delight in punning or ribald devices (of which there are many). The patterns of heraldry live on modern flag design, sports teams' colors, military insignia, sports-car logos, and a zillion other patterns of everyday life.

Heraldic devices flourished from the mid-twelfth through the mid-seventeenth centuries, declining in the post–French Revolution purges. Michel Pastoureau busts the myth that only aristocratic families held arms: About a third of arms surviving to the present day are commoner. "They were rather like the modern business card," writes Pastoureau. "Anyone can have one but not everyone does."

The Skinny on Blazon

Like most crazes, heraldry began simply and ended in baroque excess. As more and more aristocrats adopted devices, then altered them to reflect marriages and lineage, the devices necessarily became more complex.

Shields got divvied up with stripes (called *ordinaries* or *lines of partition*, depending on how they cleaved the space),

then crowded with more *charges* (pictorial elements on a shield). Women participated in heraldry from 1180 onward, adopting the more ladylike lozenge (or diamond) shape instead of a military shield. And the heraldic device expanded beyond decoration of the basic shield to accessorization. The shield's top might sprout a *wreath*, *coronet*, or *crest* (a helmet mounted with horns and ornamental doohickeys). The shield might rest on leafy *mantling* or be positioned within a *compartment*, held up by *supporters* (animals or people who brandish the shield at either side, Vanna White–style), and finished off with a scrolling *motto*. The whole device was called, self-flatteringly enough, "the complete achievement."

Heraldry invented its own rainbow, too, divided into metals (*Or*, gold or yellow, and *Argent*, silver or white), and colors (*Gules* for red, *Azure* for blue, *Sable* for black, *Vert* for green, and *Purpure* for purple). Stylized patterns of furs—*Ermine* and *Vair*, a type of pricey squirrel—completed the color (or "tincture") alphabet. Heraldists even assigned patterns to each color, so they could be understood in black-and-white print. Horizontal stripes, for instance, stood for Azure. The biggest "rule of tincture" forbids placing a color on a color or a metal on a metal, which could hinder readability.

To describe a heraldic shield, you'd read the image like a <u>medieval viewer</u> would, in layers from the deepest background up. You start with the shield's dominant color, then move on to any major division of the shield like stripes or an overall pattern. Then you name the various charges depicted, moving left to right or top to bottom. The language of heraldry gets deliciously complex. *Bendy*: the diagonal

49

■ <u>Brutal dictators, searching for bona fides:</u> Uganda dictator Idi Amin wore plaid to symbolize his country's repression by Great Britain, à la Scotland, although his extreme brutality quashed any underdog appeal he may've tapped; see page 76.

■ <u>faintly punk-rock:</u> For the actual punk-rock adoption of plaid as a signature pattern, see page 78.

✓ <u>medieval viewer:</u> This way of seeing made stripes extra-troubling to medieval Europeans: Too often they confused what was foreground and what background. See page 47.

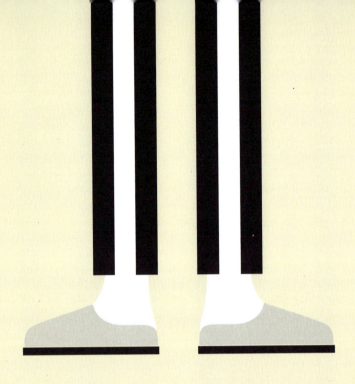

The sunlight beating on him brought out his bulk in a startling way. He made me think of a trained baby elephant walking on hind legs. He was extravagantly gorgeous too—got up in a soiled sleeping-suit, bright green and deep orange vertical stripes, with a pair of ragged straw slippers on his bare feet … You understand a man like that hasn't the ghost of a chance when it comes to borrowing clothes. Very well.

—from the novel *Lord Jim* by Joseph Conrad

stripes of caution tape. *Checky*: <u>checkerboard-pattern</u> but cuter. *Mullet*: not the haircut but a five-pointed star. *Engrailed*: scalloped. *Gyronny*: stripes radiating out from a central point. And so on.

You tack on color-names after each new element mentioned, the way French adjectives follow the noun. Thus might a heraldist describe Charlie Brown's shirt: *Or* (yellow) *a fess dancetty* (a horizontal stripe, <u>zigzagged</u>) *Sable* (the stripe is black). Where's Waldo's horizontal red-and-white-striped jersey would translate in heraldry-speak to *Barruly Argent and Gules*. (It's *barruly* because Waldo sports ten stripes on his shirt. Fewer than ten stripes, and he'd be described as *barry*.)

Heraldry gets more fun as you get more knowledgeable. Take "marks of abatement," a euphemism for blots on one's shield that denote blots on one's character like drunkenness, womanizing, or treachery. (Surprisingly, numerous heraldry books fail to answer a burning question: If heraldric devices are freely adopted by their owners, why would a nobleman ever allow one of these insulting marks on his device?) Using the rare colors *Tenny* (orange) and *Sanguine* ("blood red" or brown), heraldry can communicate volumes about nasty habits with a few simple graphics. A yellow shield dipped in brown? That's for liars. An orange square within a white shield denotes a knight who'd welched on a challenge. The most famous abatement is the "bend sinister," a diagonal stripe running from two o'clock to seven o'clock, instead of the opposite direction. It denotes a bastard family line.

Military Stripes

Springing originally from chevrons in medieval heraldry, striped insignia codify and express the military's strict hierarchy, indicating length of service, rank, and other special distinctions. Soldiers wearing striped uniforms date as far back as the fifteenth century, when German <u>mercenaries</u> or *Landsknechte* donned stripes to serve the great powers of Europe. Later uses shrank the stripes covering an entire uniform to just an insignia, often worn on the chest or shoulders. Today nearly all fighting forces across the globe have embraced a complex vocabulary of stripes. Although the systems differ in their details, generally speaking horizontally striped chevrons designate rank, while vertical stripes in different colors and widths signal individual merits the soldier has earned. Stripes as an outward expression of military hierarchy have migrated to civilian circles: "earning one's stripes" refers to any steady accumulation of experience.

More stripes usually indicates a higher honcho, with the notable exception of French sailor stripes, which mark the lowest rank-and-file. Those French sailors who rise to officer rank directly, without having attended naval school, are dismissed by their more uppity peers as "<u>zebras.</u>"

Vive la Révolution!

Stripes breezed into Enlightenment-era Europe, sweeping away previously fashionable ornate garlands and chinoiseries with a purer neoclassical style. Striped curtains, furniture,

51

■ <u>checkerboard-pattern:</u> Everything a black-and-white-checkerboard pattern can mean is covered from pages 80 to 87.

∕ <u>zigzagged:</u> The Action Jackson of dynamic patterns is discussed on page 68.

B <u>mercenaries:</u> Hired guns also played a role in the migration of Dutch wax batik patterns to West Africa. See page 15.

∕ <u>"zebras":</u> Why are zebras striped? Skip ahead to page 56 and scratch that itch already.

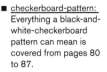

and wallpaper all strobed with refreshingly simple stripes. Stripes not only cleaned up the cluttered visual styles of the period; they also become an emblem of liberty and free thought.

During the French Revolution, stripes slashed across social hierarchies. Parisian insurgents wore red-, white-, and blue-striped rosettes, like revolutionary-floral bull's-eyes. These were pinned to long jackets with coattails, themselves in a narrow, seersucker-like stripe. The look was a nod to servants' stripes prevalent during the period and was surprisingly dashing for guillotine-heavy work.

Workers' Stripes

Hickory-striped cloth, a strong fabric of twill construction, has garbed American railroad workers since the nineteenth century. It's a diagonal <u>weave</u> of blue and white stripes, producing a vertically striped look. This weave also gives hickory exceptional durability similar to other worker twills like gabardine or denim. Hickory patterns vary to a surprising degree, with differing thicknesses of stripe and different shades of blue and creamy white. But hickory's essence always consists of vertical blue-and-white stripes on a sturdy, nubbly cloth.

The name "hickory" may derive from the fabric's strength, likened to hickory wood. In *Communicating with Pattern: Stripes*, authors Mark Hampshire and Keith Stephenson claim that the practice of calling backwoods folk "hicks" predated the cloth: "They had already been given

this derisive name—taken from the hickory canes with which less progressive rural schoolteachers used to punish their pupils." But the cloth may well have reinforced usage of the term.

Toiling outside on pancake-flat plains, laying straight railroad ties for endless miles into the horizon, these striped "hicks" streaked the country with a national infrastructure built *of* stripes.

Stripes as Male Uniform

Now let us consider the overly striped outfits of British public-school boys and the <u>tie-wearing businessmen</u> and politicians they become. Hampshire and Stephenson explain how striped school ties got their start: Oxford University students intertwined the ribbons on their boater hats, creating a striped design and thus a forerunner of striped ties. By the 1920s striped neckties dominated boys' uniforms in schools throughout England.

Once striped, always striped. Privileged schoolboys wore their alma mater's striped ties into adult life, a badge of one's affiliation in an alumni network. As Hampshire and Stephenson put it: "Indeed, it is possible to be defined by stripes right through one's life: from school tie, to college scarf, to career in the City"—the London equivalent of Wall Street.

Striped ties are one of those visual signifiers so standardized, so ubiquitous, they're open to infinite nuance. Modern men play with necktie knots and other

B <u>weave:</u> For a speedy introduction to a thousand-plus years of textile production history, see page 11.

■ <u>tie-wearing businessmen:</u> Have any tattersall-print dress shirts? Get their backstory on page 78. Argyle or plaid bow ties?

The tartan tale begins on page 72.

modifications. You can wear your striped tie loose-knotted or sharply angular, back-to-front with thin end tucked inside your shirt, radically shortened with a thick, bulky knot. The possibilities, and the subtle meanings conveyed with each style, are endless.

Seersucker

A thin cotton or rayon fabric narrowly striped in white and pale blue or other pastel shades, seersucker is perfectly cool on stifling-hot days. It's woven in such a way as to produce a slightly puckered effect, aerating the fabric while preventing it from sticking to sweaty skin. Originally made of silk and favored by British imperialists in India, the name *seersucker* stems from the Hindi phrase *śīrśakkar*, "milk and sugar," because the fabric's smooth and rough stripes resembled the smooth surface of milk and the nubbly texture of sugar.

"Widely considered patrician, seersucker was a 19th-century workingman's fabric, a cheap American cotton version of a luxurious Indian silk," according to a 2006 *New York Times* article. "In the 1920's stylish undergraduates, in a spirit of reverse snobbery, took up the thin puckered fabric for summer wear." Today those wearing seersucker transmit a willfully scrambled message about social hierarchy. Pair it with any of its classic counterparts—bow tie, straw hat, leonine Tom Wolfe-esque hair—and you've typecast yourself, consciously or not, as a Southern gentleman or Ivy League prepster. But wearing seersucker while deviating from this formula indicates a certain sartorial wit.

For a time many U.S. senators—men and women, GOP and Dems—wore the fabric on June 21 or "Seersucker Thursday." At the day's end, a pastel flotilla of spiffed-up senators would wander over to the dairy lobby's ice cream social, also held on June 21, for some wholesome bipartisan mingling. The practice started in the 1990s by the Republican senator from Mississippi Trent Lott and ended somewhat abruptly in 2012. According to the *Washington Post*, "On the evening before, the Senate cloakroom's staff notified members that the custom was being discontinued. Lott's former colleagues thought it would be politically unwise to be seen doing something frivolous when there's so much conflict over major issues." Thus an ice cream social melts away in overheated times.

Lishui and *Saek-dong*

China's Qing dynasty was populated with scuttling officials whose luxurious robes identified their rank and status with numerous details. Insignia did much of the communicating: stylized bats (bringers of happiness), flaming pearls (granters of wishes), <u>pointy scepters</u> (harbingers of prosperity), and imperial dragons whose number of claws confirmed the official's rank.

Everyone's courtly robe was edged in diagonal *lishui*, or "water wave" stripes. These were often, but not always, colored, according to the Five Phases, or *wuxing*, of East Asian cosmology: green or blue for wood, red for fire, yellow for earth, white for metal, and black for water. Each color denotes a natural process: green wood consumed by fire, whose ashes distill into earth, solidifying into metal, which enriches the water that helps wood sprout again. (Five is a magical number in East Asian Taoism. It's the number describing the complete range of senses, smells and tastes, compass directions, seasons, even martial-arts fighting moves.)

More democratically, Korean children and women wear robes with rainbow-stripy sleeves called *saek-dong* on auspicious occasions, from hundred-day-old ceremonies for babies to weddings and sixtieth birthday parties. *Saek-dong* stripes always come in the five Crayola-bright colors of *wuxing*. All five stripes together on a *saek-dong* signal cosmological completeness, protection, and the harmony of cycles.

The Animal Imaginarium

How the Tiger Got His Stripes

In February 2013 biologist Jeremy Green and his research team at King's College London answered a burning question: how tigers get their stripes. *Discovery* magazine describes how they "identified a pair of proteins called morphogens that shape the ridges on a mouse's palate. These morphogens, named fibroblast growth factor and

---

❧ <u>pointy scepters:</u> Historians have squabbled over whether the fleur-de-lis is actually an iris, lily, dove, bee, frog, or even a household or military implement. See page 103.

The tiger dies, but its stripes remain.
—Malay proverb

**The tiger's stripes are on the outside;
man's are on the inside.**
—Bhutanese proverb

sonic hedgehog, form an 'activator' and 'inhibitor' pair that together differentiate cells into ridges and troughs. The researchers believe that the same alternating chemical process stimulates skin cells to generate patches of differently colored fur."

The tiger's stripes cloak the animal with a scintillating, contradictory air. Unsurprisingly, the number-one connotation of tiger stripes is potency. The ancient Chinese revered tigers for driving off (or devouring) wild boars that threatened their crops. Tigers could even ward off demons, explaining the Chinese practices of topping graves and doorways with stone tigers, wrapping gods and heroes in protective tiger stripe, and topping children's heads with tiger caps. *The Book of Symbols*, edited by Ami Ronnberg and Kathleen Martin, describes a commonly held belief among the Chinese: "On its black forehead markings, every tiger carries a pattern identical with the Chinese character for 'king,'" a claim that illuminates the ancient Chinese refusal to say the tiger's name, *hu*, aloud. Out of hushed reverence they'd circumlocute, referring to tigers as "king of the mountains" or (somewhat oddly) "the giant reptile."

Yet all this potency radiated from a beast with, perhaps, a serious Amex problem. In the United States, according to *The Complete Dictionary of Symbols* edited by Jack Tresidder, tigers are "also an emblem of **gambling** or perhaps of its risks (a 'tiger' was slang for the lowest hand in poker in the USA)."

Tigers are also tangled up in conflicting messages, from East and West, about strong women. "Medieval bestiaries praised the 'motherly love' of the female tiger," notes *The*

Dictionary of Symbolism by Hans Biedermann. "Hunters routinely exploited her maternal instincts, placing a round **mirror** on the ground where she would look into it and mistake it for a tiger cub—which she would then attempt to nurse. (A similar ruse is proposed to save humans who are being pursued by a tigress.)" But strong maternal instinct didn't save "white tiger" from becoming a chastisement for a quarrelsome woman in Chinese.

Zebras v. Flies

Plausible evolutionary theories abound to explain the zebra's stripes: as **camouflage** (less likely than it sounds at first blush, as zebras graze in open savannahs, not in thick vegetation resembling their stripes); as displays of individual fitness (screwy stripes might indicate a less-than-robust potential mate); or as key to zebras' social interaction (each zebra boasts a print unique to itself). Still other theories suggest zebra stripes help regulate the animal's body temperature or confuse predators.

That last notion has gained traction among zoologists, whose most recent studies have circled around two members of the tabanid species, tsetse flies and horseflies. Both qualify as predators of a not-merely-irritating sort: The former causes sleeping sickness in zebras; the latter reduces body fat and milk production in horses and grazing cattle. Tabanids require a blood meal before laying eggs and reproducing, but get surprisingly finicky as to the animal's coloring they prefer. In a series of studies between 2010 and 2012, a team

● **gambling:** Turns out the pattern of dots on the five side of a die means lots of different things. See page 38.

B **mirror:** Patterns are built by repeating a motif, often with a twist like reflection across an imaginary line. For basic pattern lingo, see page 8.

● **camouflage:** Lessons in hiding oneself, from valentine puffer fish to tank battalions, begin on page 109.

of Hungarian and Swedish biologists decided to figure out why.

As actual zebras make difficult experimental subjects, the scientists kitted up a testing station on a Hungarian horse farm using inanimate objects. They arrayed side-by-side plastic trays of salad oils (to trap insects as they landed) and fake zebra models covered in glue. Some models were painted solidly dark or light-colored; others sported stripes of various widths. They put all these objects in a field infested with horseflies and counted how many insects they trapped.

The takeaway? All-black animals attracted the most flies. The bugs use reflected polarized light to guide them to egg-laying sites—and solid-dark animals, those poor fly-bitten bastards, reflect this kind of light like crazy. All-white animals repel horseflies best, although their coloring leaves them vulnerable to other threats, like skin cancer and attack by larger predators. Zebra stripes repel horseflies nearly as well as all-white coloring without some of the other drawbacks of pale hide.

Modern science robs none of the pleasure from folk tales explaining why zebras are striped, including this one from the San tribe of Namibia. An all-white zebra stumbled upon a pool of water guarded by a pushy baboon, which refused to let the zebra drink. The two animals fell into a tussle described in the children's book *How the Zebra Got His Stripes: African Folk Tales* by Cari Mostert:

> And so the fight began; backwards and forwards, this way and that, round and round, dust everywhere until with a huge kick, Zebra sent Baboon flying into the rocks of a nearby hill. Baboon landed so hard on the rough rocks that he was left with big, red, bald patches, where he had landed on his rump and they are still on his descendants to this day. Meanwhile Zebra, unbalanced by the force of his kick, had staggered into Baboon's fire, scorching his beautiful white hide, leaving him full of stripes from head to rump.

The Beast of Gévaudan

Picture this shape-shifting menace: an oversized wolf (or African hyena), sometimes described as long and squat, other times clearing three feet tall at its well-muscled shoulder. Its hurriedly glimpsed features included a "muzzle of a pig," defensive tusks like a boar, overcrowded teeth, enormous talons, sometimes fish-like scales flashing on its flanks. But every eyewitness of the beast agreed on one point: Running through bristling fur that was either rust-colored or gray, the animal's spine was always marked with a single, malicious black stripe.

During its three-year killing spree (1764–67), the Beast of Gévaudan stood accused of two hundred attacks and ninety deaths in the southern Languedoc region of France. Its preferred mode of attack was tabloid-ready: The Beast

liked to slash the jugulars of women and children tending sheep, often "eating all of her upper body down to the clavicle, but leaving the rest untouched, including the clothes." A Hollywood producer might sketch the premise thusly: "Give me Dracula meets Sasquatch, preying on sexy Little Bo Peep. But do it all French-peasant-y."

And the Beast delivered huge box-office draw. Newspaper printing presses whirred profitably with news of fresh attacks. Gun-control laws loosened, reward money piled up, and still the Beast eluded capture. Presaging the Revolution only twenty years in France's future, tales of proletariat valor in escape sprang up. In 1765, goaded by ridicule of the Crown's ineffectiveness in the matter, King Louis XV sent master hunter Antoine to kill the Beast. Antoine swept in, organized the local yokels into hunting parties, and got into a brawl with local innkeeper Jean Chastel. Chastel was deemed in the wrong and tossed into prison. With Chastel removed from action, Beast attacks suddenly dipped, suggesting to overactive imaginations that Chastel was, in fact, the werewolf-murderer. When Antoine felled a sixty-kilogram wolf with a huge stripe that September, its body was squired off to Versailles to be stuffed and publicly displayed as the Beast. Much like the groaning tables of cocaine and guns staged for press conferences in *The Wire*, the stuffed Beast served as Louis XV's "dope on the damn table." However, the carnage resumed and persisted through June 1767, when the maligned commoner Chastel supposedly plugged the animal for real. Thus ended the killing streak of a <u>terrible, black-striped Beast</u>.

Signs & Semaphores

<u>Why Are Barber's Poles Striped?</u>

The answer best combining accuracy with dishiness comes from *The History of Signboards From the Earliest Times to the Present Day*, a book coauthored by Jacob Larwood and John Camden Hotten and published in 1866.

Larwood and Hotten toured Victorian London, cataloging eye-catching signage wherever they found it. The book reads like a proto-Tumblr: a magpie collection of images, deliciously curated and captioned. Back then, barbers offered three services: hair cutting, tooth extraction, and bloodletting. Here's how Larwood and Hotten explain the striped barber's pole:

> The BARBER'S POLE . . . dates from the time that barber's practiced phle-botomy: the patient undergoing this operation had to grasp the pole in order to make the blood flow more freely . . . . As the pole was of course liable to be stained with blood, it was painted red;

/ <u>terrible, black-striped Beast:</u> To learn more about spotted panthers, turn to page 30.

when not in use, barbers were in the habit of suspending it outside the door with the white linen swathing-bands twisted round it; this, in latter times, gave rise to the pole being painted red and white.

Brewer's Dictionary of Phrase and Fable makes only slight corrections and additions to Larwood and Hotten's facts:

> The pole represents the staff gripped by persons in venesection, which was painted red since it was usually stained with blood. The white spiral represents the bandage that was twisted round the arm before bloodletting began.

Larwood and Hotten enjoy a few hilarious asides about barbers' signage above and beyond the striped pole. Some signs played off barbers' reputation for loquaciousness. One French barber near the Sorbonne in Paris placed a forbidding sign in Greek in his shop window. When translated, the sign read: "I shear quickly and am silent."

Many nineteenth-century barbers lured customers with a combination beloved by hipsters today in Brooklyn's Williamsburg section: beer and a shave. Consider this barber slogan, punning off the word "cut" as slang for "drunk":

> Rove not from pole to pole—the man lives here,

Whose razor's only equal'd by his beer;
And where, in either sense, the Cockney-put,
May, if he please, get confounded cut.

The barber's striped pole proves that, when it comes to "reading" patterns, strict fact is only a starting point. Rather it's the pole around which fantastical lore spools—much like the pole's revolving ribbons.

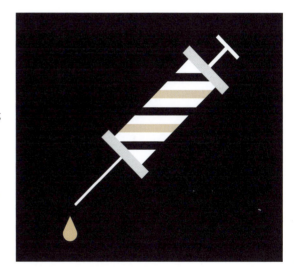

Bar Codes

"Had [N. Joseph] Woodland not been a Boy Scout, had he not logged hours on the beach, and had his father not been quite so afraid of organized crime, the bar code would very likely not have been invented in the form it was, if at all." With this chain of what-ifs, the *New York Times* obituary of Woodland put a human face on the ultimate striped abstraction: Universal Product Codes, or UPC.

As an undergraduate, N. Joseph Woodland perfected a system to record elevator music in a more efficient way—but his father put the kibosh on the project. Pop Woodland was convinced the Mob controlled elevator music, so he steered his son well clear of that. Woodland then tried encoding product data, holing up at his grandparents' Miami Beach house to consider the problem. His boyhood fascination with Morse code bubbled up at an apposite moment.

"What I'm going to tell you sounds like a fairy tale," Mr. Woodland told *Smithsonian* magazine in 1999, as quoted in the *New York Times* obituary. "I poked my four fingers into the sand and for whatever reason I pulled my hand toward me and drew four lines. I said: 'Golly! Now I have four lines, and they could be wide lines and narrow lines instead of dots and dashes.'"

Originally circular, each rectangular bar code is segmented into 95 vertical stripes that the computer reads as 0s or 1s, yielding a 95-character-long number string. (A fat black stripe consists of multiple 1s in a row, a broad white stripe a profusion of 0s.) Built-in safeguards tell the computer which ends of the number string are left and right,

so the code is legible even upside-down. The first thicket of stripes encodes what kind of product this is (pharmacy item, weighted product like fruit or meat, et cetera). The second thicket captures the manufacturer's name; the final thicket captures the exact product.

Stripey bar codes ruled until the advent of checkered Quick Response (QR) codes, which—because they encode information in two dimensions versus one-dimensional bar codes—can store much greater detail. QR codes proliferated during a honeymoon period of scan-happy smartphone users, but the practice has largely run its course. Fittingly, the QR code's final home may be cemeteries. In certain cemeteries from Japan to Seattle to Uruguay, the bereaved can scan a QR code on any headstone to learn more about the deceased.

The Structure of Iki

Stripes zip into the picture from another angle in the Japanese concept of *iki* and its manifesto *The Structure of Iki* (1929), written by Kuki Shūzō during his expat years in Paris. In this essay Shūzō defines a uniquely Japanese concept of beauty. Much like the distinctly French concept of *chic* and the German idea of *Sehnsucht* (longing), Japanese iki is grounded in seductiveness (*bitai*) but embraces other culturally specific charms, like *ikiji* ("brave composure") and *akirame* ("resignation").

Donning one's <u>secret-adolescent goggles</u>, it's easy to read *The Structure of Iki* as a "hot or not" list of Japanese aesthetics, a grab bag of turn-ons with the plausible deniability of an academic work. Willow trees; bare feet; slow, steady rain; thin fabrics; a lower-pitched female voice; the nape of a woman's neck laid bare; and vertical stripes—all signal the qualities of iki in spades. By contrast, Shūzō sniffed at desperately showy, low-iki attractions like direct lighting; bright colors (he favored muted grays, blues, and browns); heavy makeup; hair styled ornately with oil, not simply with water; and wavy or horizontal stripes.

Striped Kente Cloth

Message-driven clothing is a roomy continuum. At the low-rent, machine-washable end of the spectrum you have T-shirts bearing sayings like "My other husband is normal" and "Eat dessert first—life is uncertain." At the high-concept, damn-near-priceless, ultra-literary end, you'll find kente cloth by the Asante and Ewe peoples of Ghana.

Each kente pattern encodes a well-known saying, so you can <u>wear the perfect message for any occasion</u>. For example, say you've bumped heads with someone while planning a mutual friend's birthday party. You might wear a kente to the event to apologize for your occasional bossiness: "Sooner or later one strays into the path of another." Similar to the maxim "to err is human," this motto reminds the viewer to be conciliatory when offended, because sooner or later you'll offend someone yourself. (This kente pattern consists of diagonal stripes of gold, black, and green, arranged to meet in a V shape.)

Traditional kente is woven in silk, one hand-sized square at a time, using complicated techniques that require picking up individual threads one at a time. Each precious square is then hand-stitched together into a stripe-heavy, formal patchwork. Asante kings piled up kente in ancestral storage rooms, complete with a kente librarian who ensured the king never repeated a pattern at any public appearance. Today kente can occasionally be spotted in the United States emblazoning the cummerbunds of African-American groomsmen and the necks of graduating seniors, who favor it in bright, cassock-like scarves.

Communicating via kente is a devilishly subtle business. Consider *sika fre mogya*, a field of broad horizontal stripes interrupted with floating rectangles of tighter vertical stripes and tiny diamond shapes. It means "money attracts blood"—that is, if you're wealthy your relatives will flock to you. According to a Smithsonian exhibition about kente,

63

● secret-adolescent goggles: Calling French people "frogs" is a distinctly adolescent jab with a deep backstory; see page 104.

● wear the perfect message for any occasion: "Saying it with flowers" is a Literal Thing in floral textiles throughout the world. Learn about Turkish oya on page 108, East African kanga on page 107, and lamba hoany from Madagascar on page 108.

Once you can accept the universe as being
something expanding into an infinite nothing
which is something, wearing stripes with
plaid is easy.

—ALBERT EINSTEIN

"by wearing this cloth to a wedding you are stating that your relative is hard-working and has the means to support his new family"—not, as one might cluelessly suppose, that your famously sponging Uncle Carl better step off as you approach the wedding buffet.

Moving through the crowd at a formal Ghanaian occasion means navigating a teeming babble of kente cloth. Consider that fellow, a retired general whose quiet magnetism attracts crowds. His kente is named for the babadua tree, a tough material used for building fences and thatched roof frames. (The horizontal orange, green, and red stripes resemble stacks of felled babadua trees.) Sweeping past him might be a self-made philanthropist and a sour-faced gossip columnist, whose respective kentes silently spar. On the philanthropist: black, gold, and green diagonal stripes slanting backward, *fa hia kotwere agyeman* or "lean your poverty on Agyeman." Originally this pattern evoked an unusually generous king of the Asante Empire, Agyeman. This pattern took on a more cynical reading during the nineteenth century, when waves of village farmers fled poverty to serve in the king's court. Many former bumpkins amassed enough wealth to run for coveted "stool" positions—essentially court officials. Their arrogance gave rise to another kente pattern the gossip columnist wears as a rebuke to parvenus: *wonya wo ho a, wonye dehyee*, "you may be rich, but you're not a royal."

Certain kente are more special than others. On the day he was released from prison in 1951, Kwame Nkrumah wore the *mmeeda* kente, an evenly spaced checkerboard of wide stripes in alternating directions. Nkrumah chose mmeeda that day to say what every heart-in-mouth Ghanaian was feeling, that this historic event was "something that had not happened before." Ghana gained its independence from Britain under Nkrumah's leadership in 1957, and he became the country's first president in 1960. Nkrumah repeatedly wore kente at public events to beam various messages to the Ghanaian people. To wave from a balcony at the announcement of Ghana's independence, Nkrumah wore *adwini asa*. This complex pattern manages to convey success at both its most practical and its most giddily transcendental: it means both "I have done my best" and "all the motifs have been used up."

War & Whimsy

Dazzle Warships

In 1917 German U-boats successfully torpedoed twenty-three British ships every week—fifty-five in one week in

April alone. British navy lieutenant Norman Wilkinson proposed a solution surprisingly jazzy for a sober-sided military man: "dazzle" camouflage, a sort of large-scale zebra striping in black and white. Wilkinson explained the concept in his autobiography:

> Since it was impossible to paint a ship so that she could not be seen by a submarine, the extreme opposite was the answer—in other words, to paint her, not for low visibility, but in such a way as to break up her form and thus confuse a submarine officer as to the course on which she was heading.

Submarine shooters needed to estimate a ship's direction, speed, and location to calculate exactly where to shoot. Dazzle paint, Wilkinson hoped, would throw off these estimates, increasing the odds an enemy torpedo would miss its target.

Allied navies took to dazzle keenly, testing patterns on miniature boats in simulated conditions before daubing up a full-sized fleet. By the end of World War I, the Americans had clad 1,256 merchant ships in dazzle and claimed less than one percent of them had fallen victim to German attack.

Anecdotal evidence, at least, suggested that dazzle actually worked. "It was not until she was within half a mile," reported one U-boat captain later, "that I could make out she was one ship steering a course at right angles, crossing from starboard to port. The dark painted stripes on her after part made her stern appear her bow, and a broad cut of green paint amid ships looks like a patch of water. The weather was bright and visibility good; this was the best camouflage I have ever seen."

Still, even at the zenith of dazzle's popularity, scoffers abounded, even at the highest levels of command. Proof was shaky at best. Where dazzle and camouflage were unquestionably effective was in morale.

In World War I's aftermath, dazzle symbolized victory, jazz, and the sophistication of a triumphantly mechanical age. Here's the *London Times* describing a March 1919 costume ball in which everyone wore dazzle-patterned dress:

> Here it seemed was a token, unmistakable if bizarre, of some of the things

zebra striping: For an explanation of actual zebra striping, see page 56.

camouflage: As chapters in military history go, the tale of camouflage is much weirder and more baroque than you might expect. See page 109.

Captain Schmidt at the periscope
You need not fall and faint,
For it's not the vision of drug or dope,
But only the dazzle-paint.
And you're done, you're done, my pretty Hun.
You're done in the big blue eye,
By painter-men with a sense of fun,
And their work has just gone by.
Cheerio!
A convoy safely by.

—from a song by Gordon Frederic Norton, 1918

which the dark years had achieved
. . . To the strains of the Jazz band
these amazing revelers, vanishing and
reappearing, seemed to set at naught
the world of the past and all the
portentousness of it. They hailed a new
world, swifter, gayer, more adventurous.

It's a fitting irony: The pattern designed to hide
ship convoys was embraced by what would become the
Lost Generation.

Zigzags

Duck the whizzing bullets to consider, from a quiet foxhole,
the history of the zigzag. As a textile pattern, zigzag borders
or rows of small triangles have long been thought to ward
off danger. Eastern European women traditionally weave
"wolves' teeth" into their shawls' edges to scare off the
evil eye, just as peoples in the Golden Triangle area of
Southeast Asia did. Throughout the Muslim world textiles
are bedecked with protective triangles; often those triangles
are pouches stuffed with magically potent materials like salt,
coal, or Koranic verses scribbled on paper.

Not that zigzags only play defense. On the offense side
of things, consider the adinkra symbol *nkyinkyim*, a zigzag
widened to fill a horizontal rectangular space. Among the
Asante people of Ghana, nkyinkyim stands for versatility,
initiative, and dynamism.

The word *zigzag* first popped up in France in 1712 as
"zic-zac," a gardening term for paths formed of short lines
at alternating angles. The term took on another meaning in
1733: According to the *Oxford English Dictionary*, it referred
to a "fortification. A trench leading towards a besieged place,
constructed in a zigzag direction so as not to be enfiladed by
the defenders."

Having acquired a dashing military air, "Zig-Zag"
was an ideal brand name for tobacco papers, interleaved
in a zigzag pattern, and introduced in 1894. The name
purportedly gave homage to a French soldier known only
as "le Zouave," who coolly produced a clay pipe for a
smoke during the battle of Sevastopol—only to see the
pipe exploded into shards by a stray bullet. Undeterred, le
Zouave tore a jagged piece of paper from a gunpowder bag
and coolly rolled his tobacco with that.

Linguistically, "zigzag" falls into a category of terms
called "reduplications." (Why it's not merely a "duplication"
is unclear—although it's possibly a linguist's in-joke,
a pun on the phenomenon it's naming.) Well-known
reduplications include "knick-knack," "namby-pamby,"
and "helter-skelter"; more obscure zoological variants
include "horny-dorny" (another name for a snail) and
"marly-scarly" (caterpillar). A Hungarian cousin of the term
"zigzag" is *zeg-zug*, which translates to "nooks and crannies"
in American parlance.

"Striped Paint"

If you went searching, as many construction-site newbies have, for a can of striped paint, you'd find it in a closet full of other fool's-errand bait: the left-handed screwdriver, the tub of elbow grease, the board-stretchers atop a box of assorted <u>knots</u>. It's stuffed in the same closet with golden rivets (much sought after by new navy men), turn signal fluid (auto mechanics), and coils of fallopian tubing (medical students).

Candy Canes

How candy canes got their red-and-white stripes is a tale in which slender fact is wrapped in a cotton-candy-like gauze of theory. The *Oxford English Dictionary* dates the first appearance of "candy cane" or "candy-striped" in print to the late 1800s, yet *Introduction to Food Science* calmly insists that, "In 1670, the choirmaster at the Cologne Cathedral gave sugar sticks to his young singers to keep them quiet during the long Living Crèche ceremony. In honor of the occasion, he had the candies bent into the shepherds' crooks." In a similar, treacly vein, other sources describe an anonymous candy maker from Indiana who purportedly fashioned the candy cane as a Christian symbol down to its last detail: its pure white body symbolizing Jesus's sinless birth, its J-for-Jesus shape, and its red stripes representing the bloody scourging Jesus endured to redeem humanity.

All these maybes "explaining" the candy cane's provenance harden into facts at the U.S. Patent Office. Enter Patent U.S. 2956520 A, granted in 1960, for a "candy cane forming machine," designed to receive "straight sticks of candy while in a semi-plastic state and . . . [bend] the ends of the sticks into crooks . . . by a rolling action, whereby complete control with little or no breakage is attained." Its author was both a pragmatic capitalist and a man of the cloth, Father Gregory H. Keller. He produced the machine for his brother-in-law Bob McCormack of Bobs Candies, now part of Ferrara Candy Company, the nation's largest producer of candy canes (not to mention conversation hearts, jelly beans and 92 percent of the U.S. mallowcreme market).

Impressive as the candy cane forming machine may be, its technological triumph is dwarfed by "Blackpool rock," a striped candy common in Blackpool and other English resort towns. A stick of hard-boiled sugar also flavored with mint, the miracle of "rock" cracks open only when you bite it. Inside the stick, you'll see bright lettering spelling out the name of the seaside vacationland where you bought it. Bite after bite, the same letters appear—a marvel accomplished via artfully placed horizontal stripes of colored sugar, forming the letters in transverse.

¬ <u>knots:</u> Unraveling knotted patterns is a deeper business than one might suppose. See page 122.

Squares

Checks

The Full Macgillicuddy About Tartan

Early Plaids

Chaotic yet orderly, clashingly exuberant, the story lines meeting in tartan's history jumble fact with sometimes outrageous fiction. Nearly everything you think you "know" about tartan was invented, then furiously believed until fact seemed pale and unsporting in comparison.

First, to vocabulary: "tartan" refers to a category of twill-weave patterns consisting of two sets of stripes at right angles to each other. An individual tartan—with its recipe of color palette and specific stripe widths—is called a "sett." In Gaelic, a *plaide* refers to any woolen blanket, tartan-patterned or not. Honoring the American tradition of <u>linguistic loosey-gooseyness</u>, the terms "tartan" and "plaid" will from here out be considered interchangeable.

The oldest known Scottish tartan, the Falkirk sett, dates from the third century C.E. (So impossible was it for scholars to imagine that tartan might *not* originate in Scotland that older, tartan-ish scraps, when discovered in Scandinavia and Xianjiang, China, sent academics on a plaid-goose-chase, trying—and largely failing—to establish some ancient Gaelic-Chinese contact.)

Ancient Scots wore a three-piece tartan ensemble: a *léine*, or tunic-shirt; a *brat*, a semi-circular cloak; and <u>tight-fitting hotpants</u> called *trews*. By the seventeenth century, this getup evolved into the *fhéilidh-Mor*, or belted plaid. Scots

---

⟋ <u>linguistic loosey-</u>
⌐ <u>gooseyness:</u> The word *stripe* in several languages is etymologically related to words for punishment, deprivation, or outright

deletion. See page 48. "Pattern poets" arranged their verses on the page to make patterns pleasing to both the ear and eye. See page 120.

● <u>tight-fitting hotpants:</u> For more on skimpy clothing, see the history of the ever-shrinking bikini (and why it's so often polka-dotted) on page 28.

would place a belt on the ground and the plaid blanket on top of it. You'd pleat the plaid at right angles to the belt, then lie down on it, pull the plaid's edges around yourself, belt it into place, and stand up a fully kilted Scotsman. Below the belt, a loosely pleated skirt would skim your knees; above it, you'd have swags of tartan fabric that could be arranged into a <u>shawl</u>. This versatile garment also doubled as a sleeping bag when traveling. The ladies wore a longer version of the belted plaid, called the *arisaid*. Other accessories included the *sporran*, a tasseled bag worn around the waist; a *skean-dhu*, or sheathed dagger tucked into a kneesock; and brogans, a style of high-ankled boot.

So far, so indisputably true. Heavy myth-making about tartan starts with who adapted the belted plaid into the "little kilt," or *fhéilidh beag*, predominant today. Over the partisan complaint of some scholars, the facts suggest it was an English industrialist, Thomas Rawlinson, who opened an iron-smelting factory in 1727 in Invergarry, stocking it with local Scottish employees. "Observing that the traditional *fhéilidh-Mor* was uncomfortably hot and dangerously impractical," writes Jonathan Faiers in *Tartan*, "Rawlinson hit upon the idea of shortening and separating the pleated lower half from the cumbersome top half." Dead sexy, as Mike Myers's Scottish character Fat Bastard might remark— and also dead practical on the factory floor.

The Squashing o' the Tartan

The story starts with centuries of unfair squabbling between the Scottish and the English. Tartan's troubles began with James VII, his Scottish title: Confusingly, he later became James II of England and reigned there from 1685 to 1688. A staunch Catholic, James VII was chased from the throne in favor of the Protestant Dutch duo William and Mary, who happened to be James's daughter and son-in-law. Grousing Scots claimed James's infant son, named James Francis Edward Stuart, was the rightful heir to the British crown. Thus began seventy years of Jacobite rebellions ("Jacobite" from the Latinate form of "James"). The Jacobites first rallied around the infant-grown-up James (somewhat dubiously nicknamed the "Old Pretender") and later around his charismatic son, Bonnie Prince Charlie, the "Young Pretender."

The bonnie prince, formally known as Charles Edward Stuart, mounted a charm offensive in 1744, raising Scottish troops to claim the English throne while appealing to the French for backup. His ragtag army enjoyed early success but lost badly at Culloden in 1746. Charles was spirited from the scene, disguised as an Irish maid by one Flora MacDonald. Even though one observer called Charles-in-drag a "very odd, muckle, ill-shapen up wife," the Young Pretender pulled the escape off, spending his remaining years anticlimactically as a maudlin drunk in France.

The English wasted no time squashing what remained of the Jacobite movement and subjugating the Scottish Highlands. They started with the Disarming Act of 1746, which banned tartan on penalty of imprisonment (strike one) and deportation (strike two). Here's an excerpt from the oath suspected tartan-wearers had to take:

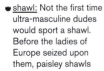
● shawl: Not the first time ultra-masculine dudes would sport a shawl. Before the ladies of Europe seized upon them, paisley shawls clothed Mughal princes; see page 95.

I do swear . . . never [to] use any tartan, plaid or any part of the Highland garb; and if I do so, may I be cursed in my undertakings, family and property—may I never see my wife and children, father, mother and relations—may I be killed in battle as a coward, and lie without Christian burial, in a strange land . . . may all this come across me if I break my oath.

During the ban, plaid-wearing became popular among the groups exempt from the ban: those in army service, women, and anyone living outside of Scotland (or in the Lowlands, where English control was more certain).

The era of plaid-wrapped nostalgia was on. Wealthy Jacobites commissioned waves of portraits, featuring themselves illicitly robed in tartan. A penny-novel version of Charles's doomed adventure sold like hotcakes. Songsters churned out innumerable ditties memorializing the uncouth, valorous, and undeniably sexy "Highland Laddie" (always garbed, in a convenient rhyme, in "tartan plaidie").

Tartan's boosters also got organized. In 1778 the Highland Society of London formed, dedicated to improving economic prospects in Scotland and preserving Gaelic language and culture. The society got the tartan ban repealed in 1782—which, far from neutralizing the craze, only increased tartan-ardor.

Tartan Washing

Cut to the 1815 tartan survey, in which the Highland Society of London asked each clan chief for a sample of their traditional sett. The survey catalogued seventy-six setts—despite most chiefs' awkward admission that they had no idea what their clan tartan might be. The connection between clan and sett had always been loose; it's much more likely that certain setts were associated with specific Highland districts than with families.

When King George IV made a formal visit to Edinburgh in 1822, the situation became urgent: how would the cheering crowds dress to greet him, if not in their families' ancestral tartan setts? A public spectacle stage-managed by novelist Sir Walter Scott, the visit was intended to celebrate Britain Unified Under a Hanoverian King and airbrush out the Highlands' subjugation seventy-five years earlier.

An adroit PR expert, Scott papered over the event's many fissures with blinding amounts of tartan. (Scott's own son-in-law dubbed the event a "Celtic hallucination.") The plaid started with the dignitaries at the center of his tableau: the permanently drunken Lord Mayor of London, Sir William Curtis, and the morbidly obese king, both of whom Scott wrapped in Royal Stewart tartan. Scott hid George's ulcerous legs in flesh-colored leggings under his kilt, to the kvelling of newspaper cartoonists across the British Isles. Amazingly, the event proved successful, the Hanoverians solidified their rule over Scotland, and yet another wave of plaid mania spread across Europe.

74

B "Celtic hallucination":
∕ Other instances of patterns playing tricks on us: the phenomenon of pareidolia (page 19) and "dazzle-painted" warships (page 65).

● kvelling of newspaper cartoonists: In 1962 a comic-book character seized on polka dots as his superhero power. See page 32.

Plaid Fraud

Both during and after the tartan ban, quite a few people conspired to manufacture myths about tartan's origins and meanings, rewriting the Scottish Highlands' history even as its clan culture was vanishing.

The year 1760 saw the "discovery" of verses by Ossian, a third-century Scottish poet lauded as the "Celtic Homer." Ossian was actually the construct of two men, both coincidentally named James Macpherson. James Macpherson #1 collected Irish ballads throughout Scotland, changed their setting from Ireland to Scotland, then demoted the original Irish songs into supposed variants of Ossian's older works. A minister from Sleat on the Isle of Skye, James Macpherson #2 produced a critical appraisal of Ossian, declaring O's work the product of Irish-speaking Celtic Scots inhabiting the Highlands *four centuries* before

the Irish got there. (Insert proud-Scotsman-slash-academic mic-drop here.) Goethe, Schubert, and Schiller not only believed in Ossian's existence, they gave him rave reviews as a poet. Napoleon snapped up an "original" Ossian edition, and Ossian-themed merch—all decorated in plaid, of course—and cultural products filled opera halls and art galleries throughout Europe.

The next wave of plaid-fraud occurred after the ban was lifted. In 1829 brothers John and Charles Allan unearthed a manuscript called the *Vestiarium Scoticum* (*The Garde-robe of Scotland*), a gift supposedly handed down to them from the Bonnie Prince Charles himself. (The Allans claimed their father Thomas was the Young Pretender's secret son.) This manuscript traced specific setts to clan families of Scotland back to 1571—quite a lot older than any previous historical record. <u>Boo-yah!</u>

The brothers dodged attempts to verify their claims while maintaining a helpful-seeming front. Their list of my-dog-ate-my-tartan excuses was long and plausible. When doubts encircled them, the brothers converted to Roman Catholicism and changed their name again to Sobieski Stuart, after the Polish royal family related to the Young Pretender. The Sobieski Stuarts established a home full of dubious Scottish relics in Inverness, where they published a luxurious limited edition of the *Vestiarium Scoticum* in 1842. They followed this with *Costume of the Clans*, a less contentious book of tartan setts, and two years after that a collection of short stories about two brothers, grandsons to the Young Pretender, decorated by Napoleon and poised to reestablish the House of Stuart in Scotland.

🌢 <u>Boo-yah!</u>: Styling an iconic pattern as even more ancient than previously supposed is a classic power move. Proto-Frankish King

Pharamond on page 105 offers a prime example.

It's one thing to fake scholarship "proving" what everyone would love to believe; it's another to threaten the reigning British crown in thinly veiled fiction. Once they'd overreached into treason, the big hook of public opinion settled around the Sobieski Stuarts' shoulders and escorted them off stage-right. Their legacy isn't entirely besmirched, though: Their scholarship was bunkum, but the interest the Sobieski Stuarts encouraged in Highland culture cannot be argued.

What Do Scots Wear Under That Kilt?

The Edwardian era (1901–1910) saw the rise of men's business suits in England, a uniform that became subsequently so universal in the West, it rendered any deviations in male dress as impossibly exuberant. "Exuberant" being often a euphemism for "gay," men wearing kilts tended to crank up the testosterone to fend off this superstition. During World War I, the Germans called kilted Scottish soldiers "ladies from Hell."

Dozens of films and cartoons have wondered what Scots wear under their kilts. But none milked the question so insistently for laughs as Laurel and Hardy's film *Putting Pants on Philip* (1927). Laurel plays Philip, the Scottish nephew of Piedmont Mumblethunder (played by Hardy). Philip wears a succession of tartan kilts while visiting his uncle in the States. He's also prone to jump up, alarmingly raising the kilt, every time he spots a pretty woman. This gag happens umpteen times, eventually revealing that Philip is wearing American-style boxer shorts under there. The underwear-coast seems clear—until Philip sneezes violently, dropping his drawers while he stands, Marilyn Monroe–style, over a subway vent. "This dame ain't got no lingerie on," barks a passing policeman while ladies swoon. Uncle Mumble-thunder finally frog-marches Philip to the tailor's to be fitted for pants.

The Revolution Will Be Tartanized

The erratic Ugandan dictator Idi Amin felt a kinship between his country and Scotland, both of which had been subjugated under England's imperial thumb. After staging a coup in 1971, Amin briefly clothed his troops in Royal Stewart tartan kilts. He also liked to declare himself the "uncrowned King of Scotland" (along with other deluded titles like "Conquerer of the British Empire" and "His Excellency President for Life"). Poke whatever fun you like at Amin's tartan getup; his legacy stops humor cold. He was responsible for killing nearly a half-million of his fellow citizens, and the *Guardian*'s obituary for Amin in 2003 strikes an unusually definitive note: "Amin brought bloody tragedy and economic ruin to his country, during a selfish life that had no redeeming qualities."

Back in 1970s Blighty, well-fed punks were shredding up tartans, sticking nappy-pins through their noses, and generally shitting on every Establishment England

∕ men's business suits:
How did striped ties become The Thing among male executives? Turn to page 52.

As if in divine confirmation of my train of thought, when Idi stood up for the vows, he was wearing a kilt. The sea-green jacket was just part of the Highland get-up, spats and sporran, skean-dhu and brogans . . . the full, romantic, nonsensical lot, the same as I had seen in the mountains.

—**from** *The Last King of Scotland* **by Giles Foden**

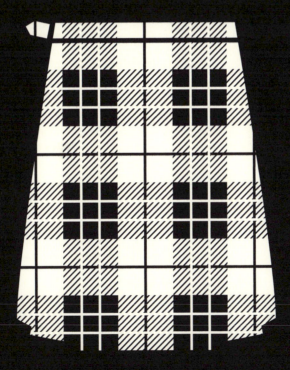

signifier they could find. "It is with Vivienne Westwood and Malcolm MacLaren's launch of Seditionaries, the last of their retail incarnations . . . in late 1976, that tartan becomes indelibly associated with punk," writes Jonathan Faiers in his book *Tartan*. Westwood pushed tartan to high-rent fashionistas enamored of punk (and immune to irony).

Name-checking the Famous Checks

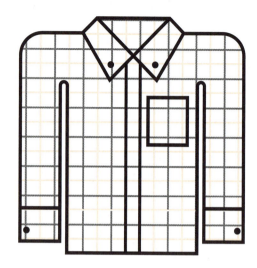

Tattersall

This natty four-square pattern on men's dress shirts is named for Richard Tattersall, founder of the world's first bloodstock auction house for horses in 1766. Write the authors of *Communicating with Pattern: Squares, Checks and Grids*: "Various sources attribute the checked pattern to the blankets his horses wore when they were taken to the market." The pattern migrated from horse blankets to the weekend garb of well-heeled London businessmen. Tattersall's still sells five thousand <u>thoroughbred horses</u> annually, all priced traditionally in shillings, not pounds.

⟋ thoroughbred horses:
Gambling and its often
ruinous costs are also
symbolized by tigers. See
page 56.

Gingham

An honest, practical checkerboard made of red-and-white squares, gracing picnic tables and cozy Italian eateries. Gingham was first named for the weave, a simple twill whose even spacing of <u>warp and weft</u> colors produced no "right" or "wrong" side. <u>Originating in the East and popularized in the West</u> in Holland, blue-and-white gingham enriched textile manufacturers in the city of Manchester, England in the eighteenth century, then leapfrogged the Atlantic Ocean where Southerners in America churned out massive quantities of the cloth.

In France, gingham goes by a tonier name, "vichy," for the French city dominating its manufacture. Just as hardwearing, cheerful, and thrifty to French consumers as to Americans, vichy has exploded in visibility in the modern era on *totes Barbès*, an inexpensive plastic totebag printed in pink-and-blue gingham. (Look around any thoroughfare, subway car, or DMV waiting room: guaranteed you'll notice someone hauling a tote Barbès.) Ultralight, indestructible, easy to clean, and dead-cheap, totes Barbès are hands-down the world's most popular, most practical luggage.

Why are totes Barbès so often printed in a gingham pattern? "Vichy" dominates the branding for Tati, a French discount department store. Tati printed this pattern on supercheap shopping totes they manufactured and sold, first in the neighborhoods of Paris populated by Berbers and other North African immigrants, but now—in original and knockoff versions—throughout the world.

Houndstooth

A broken check made of abstracted, four-point shapes, traditionally in black-and-white. Houndstooth's origins are hazy, but earliest wearers were probably shepherds in the Scottish Highlands, who liked how splashed mud wasn't too noticeable on houndstooth outerwear. As the name implies, "houndstooth" got its name from its resemblance to the jagged back teeth of hunting hounds, although the pattern also goes by other names: "shepherd's plaid," "four-in-four check," "gun club check," and (adorably) "puppytooth" when it's smaller in scale. To the French it's called *pied de poule*, "chicken foot."

Houndstooth climbed up the social ladder when English gentry adopted it as sensible but natty hunting wear. It got another boost when Edward, Duke of Windsor (he of Wallis-Simpson-throne-abdicating fame) started using houndstooth as a formal suiting material, far from the mucky fens of the English countryside. The world—enamored of his <u>ballsiness both sartorially and personally</u>—followed his lead. Houndstooth went thoroughly *Upstairs, Downstairs* by midcentury: Christian Dior made the pattern synonymous with haute couture, even as below-stairs cooks made houndstooth the preferred pattern of food-splattered chef's pants.

B <u>warp and weft:</u> Your primer in basic textile lingo starts on page 8.

<u>Originating in the East</u>
B <u>and popularized in the West:</u> Two other patterns followed a similar trade route. Paisley originated as a shawl pattern for Mughal princes before

taking the West by storm in the nineteenth century; see page 95. Dutch wax batik is another tangled example of how far patterns can wander from their birthplace and even

become emblematic of an entirely foreign culture. See page 15.

<u>ballsiness both sartorially and personally:</u> Another cool customer associated with pattern was a French soldier known only as "le Zouave." See page 68.

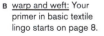

All the World in Black & White

say, in Australia or Brunei; only in Chicago and environs do cops wear Sillitoe tartan proper. Pittsburgh police wear a version in black-and-gold checkerboard.)

Sir Percy first introduced his tartan in 1931 to improve police visibility. Sillitoe tartan enjoyed greater traction than the more poncy alternate idea, that cops flounce about in white capes. Spreading outward from Glasgow, Sillitoe tartan had blanketed the entire British police force by 1974.

Law & Order

Like an undercover spy, the black-and-white checkerboard pattern goes by many work names. Among police the world over, it's known as Sillitoe tartan. Named for one Sir Percy Sillitoe, a Glasgow police chief who rose to director of Britain's elite MI5 secret service, Sillitoe tartan trims the uniforms of coppers throughout the former British Commonwealth. (Adoption in the United States is spottier than,

Percy's other wins as police chief included introducing wireless communications among patrol cars and putting down the intractable Glasgow "razor gangs."

Sillitoe's autobiography *Cloak Without Dagger* details his reluctant rise as director of MI5 from 1946 to 1953. Much like the fictional George Smiley of John le Carré fame, Sillitoe battled a series of high-level Soviet moles within MI5 as the Cold War chilled everything around him. Lurking among their numbers was one Klaus Fuchs, a nuclear physicist who managed to evade him and hand over the secret of hydrogen bombs to the Soviet Union—an astounding gaffe no amount of Sillitoe tartan would help Sir Percy live down. Sillitoe retired from MI5 to the relaxing sinecure of plugging holes in the illegal diamond trade for De Beers.

Logic

Traditionally black-and-white, the alternating squares of a chessboard count as one of the world's most magnetic patterns, an expanse furiously contemplated over billions of hours of game play. Described in an Indian proverb as "a sea in which a <u>gnat</u> may drink and an elephant may bathe," chess originated in India in the fifth century C.E. and spread throughout the globe, morphing into its current incarnation in sixteenth-century Italy. (The simpler, more ancient game of "draughts" is also played on an eight-by-eight board of alternating squares. It took on the name "checkers" in the fourteenth century in reference to the playing board's pattern and, ultimately, to distinguish this much cruder game from chess.)

The chessboard features in one of the oldest fables among mathematicians. Dubbed the wheat or rice problem, the story illustrates the <u>principle of geometric progression</u>. A shah in ancient Persia was so impressed by the game of chess, he summoned its inventor to his palace and granted him any wish he could name. A poor peasant with a deadly firm grasp of numbers, the inventor asked only for the amount of wheat necessary to fill a chessboard like so: starting on the first square, place one grain of wheat, then double the amount on the previous square until the board is filled. Bowled over by this humble-sounding request, the shah busied a servant straightaway with the task. The burden was modest along the checkerboard's first row; but the obligation grew at an alarming clip from there. By the end, the entire chessboard should be theoretically full of 18 *quintillion*-plus grains of wheat, equivalent to 150 times the current global annual production of the grain. As Carl Sagan observed about the fable: "Exponentials can't go on forever, because they will gobble up everything."

Good and Evil

In a more cosmic-accounting vein, a black-and-white checked fabric in Bali called *wastra poleng* represents the opposing forces of good and evil, light and dark, that keep the world balanced. The Balinese drape wastra poleng liberally over any object or person with a protective function:

81

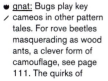

● <u>gnat</u>: Bugs play key cameos in other pattern tales. For rove beetles masquerading as wood ants, a clever form of camouflage, see page 111. The quirks of horseflies and tsetse flies explain why zebras are striped; see page 57.

● <u>principle of geometric progression</u>: Also from the annals of mathematical principles: Sir Francis Galton invented the quincunx box in the nineteenth century to demonstrate a principle of probability, normal distribution. See page 35.

guardian shrines, umbrellas, roadside kiosks of <u>magical healers</u>. The pattern is such a potent symbol that a local environmental non-governmental organization (NGO) was able to protect threatened Balinese forests by wrapping thousands of trees around the island in wastra poleng.

Value

Money—that necessary evil—found perhaps its ultimate checkered expression in the Indonesian island of Buton, where villagers used a specific black-and-white-checkered cloth as their currency until the mid-twentieth century. *Kampuna*, meaning "head cloth of the king," was woven on official <u>looms</u> to validate its use as currency (not to be confused with so many unvalidated picnic throws).

Speed

A minor astonishment of publishing: an entire book exists about the origins of the black-and-white-checkered racing flag. Guess what it's called? *Origin of the Checker Flag: A Search for Racing's Holy Grail*. In it, author Fred Egloff traces this symbol of speed back to the 1906 Glidden Tour, in which "checking stations" between Buffalo, New York, and Bretton Woods, New Hampshire, were marked with suitably punning checkered flags. The first race in which a checkered flag marked the finish line occurred that same year, in the 1906 Vanderbilt Cup.

That's the closest brush one can make with the facts. But the race to explain the checkered flag's origins kicks up a lot of apocryphal theories, too. Nascar.com offers two common ones. First, back in the racing-horse-and-buggy days, races often ended with everyone companionably tucking into a meal. Waving a black-and-white-<u>checkered tablecloth</u>, therefore, made it clear when it was time to break for chow. Second, theories explaining any distinctive pattern nearly always include a Visibility Argument. The checkered racing flag punched through the dusty haze, clearly demarcating the finish line.

An *Indianapolis Star/News* reporter advanced a few more explanations in a 1999 article: perhaps race officials, wearing checkered vests, stationed themselves at key points along the route to mark the course. Or possibly a "flamboyant or thoughtful" official donned a fully black-and-white checkered suit and stood at the finish line: an unmissable marker for tuckered-out contestants. Finally, there's a tale of a "boneshaker" bicycle race, held in Paris in 1964, where a race official may have waved a checkered scarf, loaned to him by a snappily dressed spectator. From tablecloths to vests to suits to scarves, those checks have run their own speedy course through lore.

Kaffiyeh

Kaffiyeh refers to the rectangular cotton-wool headscarf worn by Arab men, in a check variously described as "chain-link," "dogtooth," or "knotted net." You fold a kaffiyeh diagonally, drape it over the head, and hold it in place with a head rope (*agal*).

● <u>magical healers</u>: Bushmen healers in Africa induce hallucinogenic trips and then record their visions in dot-addled rock paintings. See page 32.

B <u>looms</u>: For a breakneck recap of textile production history, see page 11.

■ <u>checkered tablecloth</u>: Gingham also pops up frequently on picnic tablecloths. For the backstory of this pattern, see page 79.

I WANT TO BE YOUR MOTHERFUCKING
CHECKERED FLAG, RYLEE. YOUR PACE CAR
TO LEAD YOU THROUGH TOUGH TIMES,
YOUR PIT STOP WHEN YOU NEED A BREAK,
YOUR START LINE, YOUR FINISH LINE,
YOUR GODDAMN VICTORY LANE.

—from the novel *Crashed*
by K. Bromberg

The *kaffiyeh* (plural *kuffiyaat*) first rose to prominence in 1936, when Palestinians rebelled against Jewish immigration under the British Mandate. With a kaffiyeh draped around the neck in a loose triangle (a style called *shemagh*), a rebel could quickly hide his face from an onslaught of gritty wind—or from identification by Israeli combatants. By 1938, Palestinian rebels commanded everyone, civilian or fighter, to wear kuffiyaat regularly, so that guerrillas could vanish into crowds undetected. Wearing an Ottoman fez—the preferred headgear of upper-class Palestinians—now signaled opposition to the rebels and was strongly frowned upon.

Kuffiyaat swung back into the public eye in the 1960s. Yasser Arafat, chairman of the Palestine Liberation Organization (PLO) and leader of the Fatah political party, wore his black-and-white kaffiyeh habitually, draping it over his right shoulder to approximate Palestine's shape. (Red-and-white kuffiyaat signal the wearer's association with Socialist factions or Hamas; black-and-white kuffiyaat indicate allegiance to Fatah.)

The kaffiyeh's popularity really surged when worn by Leila Khaled, fighter for the Popular Front for the Liberation of Palestine (PFLP). In a now-iconic photo, she's cradling a Kalashnikov, delicate head turned away, her dark pixie-cut hair draped in a black-and-white kaffiyeh. (When asked about a ring she wore in the photo, Khaled told the *Guardian*: "I made it from the pin of a hand grenade—from the first grenade I ever used in training. I just wrapped it around a bullet." Call it <u>Etsy Commando-Style</u>.)

Khaled hijacked her first plane at age twenty-five in 1969, then got <u>six cosmetic surgeries on her face</u>, *sans* anesthesia, just so she could elude recognition and hijack again. The following year, she boarded a plane with a Honduran passport and a grenade in each pocket ("only to threaten," Khaled told the *Guardian*. "I did not want to blow up the plane."). The flight was diverted to London, and she deplaned, alive, into the deeply unamused embrace of Ealing police. Authorities later traded Khaled for Western hostages held by the PFLP.

Focused, ruthlessly principled, and <u>smokin' hot</u>, Khaled wrapped in kaffiyeh became a pinup girl for Palestinian liberation and unruly youth everywhere. One imagines Khaled's reaction to the questionable homage of Leela, Doctor Who's sexy sidekick in the 1975 movie: heavy-lidded, humorless stare through a dense wall of cigarette smoke. (Khaled wrapped herself in smoke as often, and as tenderly, as in her kaffiyeh. She dryly characterized a boring period in her youth like so: "I was politically conscious and a chain smoker—I needed no other diversions.")

Kuffiyaat popped up in Japan in the late 1980s, slithering around the necks of trendy teens. In 2007, in the teeth of the second Iraq War, Urban Outfitters started selling suspiciously kaffiyeh-like "antiwar woven scarves," then yanked them from the shelves due to public outcry—a clash of why-you-wanna-look-like-a-terrorist? and who-you-*calling*-a-terrorist? Dunkin' Donuts similarly fell afoul of public opinion with a commercial featuring Rachael Ray, kaffiyeh-clad, strolling like a smug New York University student with her Coffee Coolata. Taking appropriation to the next level, SemiticSwag. com now sells a sky-blue-and-white kaffiyeh sprinkled with

- **Etsy Commando-Style:** Military camouflage started as a homespun affair that scaled to industrial grade within just a few decades. See page 114.
- **six cosmetic surgeries on her face:** A less dire intervention into one's looks, "patching" involved strategically placing moles on one's face and shoulders. See page 41.
- **smokin' hot:** Photographer Lee Miller posed naked and tangled in netting for a camouflage training session, while pinup girl Chili Williams illustrated camo techniques (clothed) for *Life* magazine. See page 113.

> "With my keffiyah [*sic*],
> I am home, we are united."
>
> "It's only a scarf!"
>
> —two subjects wearing kuffiyaat in
> Cultural Appropriation: A Conversation
> by UK photographer Sanaa Hamid

Stars of David, along with a rainbow kaffiyeh, camouflage kaffiyeh, American- and Brit-themed kuffiyaat—a kaffiyeh for every millennial-seeking cause.

From the kaffiyeh fashion wars, two lessons ring out clear. First: Appropriate a serious pattern lightly, and you can manage to piss off the entire political spectrum—right, left, *and* center. (Paradoxically, that pissing-off might not teach you any lessons, as your "mistake" can also grab headlines and move a lot of merch.) Second: Lest one laugh off pattern as a frivolous subject, kaffiyeh proves just how charged, how meaning-packed, a pattern can be.

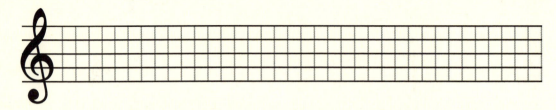

I'm not interested in possible complexities.

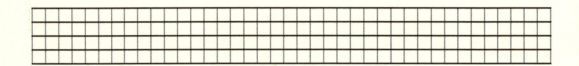

I regard song structure as a graph paper.

—MINIMALIST COMPOSER BRIAN ENO

Borders & Built Things

Adinkra Squares

The Asante people of Ghana wear a sumptuous fabric called *adinkra*. It's created by printing fine cloth with thick black dye in a <u>grid</u> (called *nkyimu*). Then, using calabashes carved with symbols, you stamp the cloth with various symbols to fill the grid in. The nkyimu grid is itself a meaningful adinkra symbol, signaling skillfulness or precision.

Two checked adinkra symbols, frequently used as borders, stand out for their opposed meanings. *Owuo atwedee* is called "ladder of death" and symbolizes mortality. A densely woven square check, called *kete pa*, means "good bed," signifying a happy marriage.

Graph Paper

An infinite calm descends while one is contemplating a clean, empty sheet of graph paper. All those empty squares, girded in a pale green or blue latticework. One receives a jolt of surprise on learning that, like the existence of <u>alternate universes</u>, there's actually more than one kind of graph paper. The classic four-square pattern is known as quad paper—short for quadrille, a square <u>dance-step</u>. Even odder is the fact that, according to Merriam-Webster's Collegiate Dictionary, the term "graph paper" is quite recent: it first appeared in print in 1927.

Considering all the kinds of graph paper dizzies the mind. There's engineering paper, usually translucent green or tan; its faint grid lines are printed on the paper's backside, so they guide the engineer's hand while drafting but don't show up in photocopies. Hexagonal paper delivers what its name promises: a surface of interlocking hexagons. Its more complicated cousin is isometric or 3-D graph paper, a pattern of sixty-degree triangles. Its uses range from future-forward 3-D renderings to throwbacks like planning trianglepoint embroidery. Logarithmic graph paper resembles a boldly asymmetrical plaid in black-and-white; the grid lines grow denser toward the upper right-hand corner of each square. Polar coordinate paper frankly blows the mind: a pale expanse like all graph paper, dominated by a concentric bull's-eye.

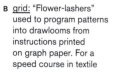

B <u>grid</u>: "Flower-lashers" used to program patterns into drawlooms from instructions printed on graph paper. For a speed course in textile production history, turn to page 11.

⌐ <u>alternate universes</u>: Patterns gird up the natural world, from the teeniest structure of crystals to turbulent weather fronts and jagged coastlines. See pages 123 and 125.

● <u>dance-step</u>: A craze for polka music ripped through Europe and America in the mid-nineteenth century, leaving a curious historical vestige in its wake: the "polka dot." See page 23.

Why Are Honeycombs Hexagonal?

Honeycombs are unnervingly precise: a machine-quality matrix of hexagons, each angle exactly 120 degrees. But why?

It's an age-old question first posed in 36 B.C.E. by Marcus Terentius Varro, a Roman soldier-scholar-writer. Varro mulled possible answers in a text now known as "The Honeycomb Conjecture." He lacked the mathematical chops to answer his own question conclusively, but he believed the <u>bees</u> had good reason for preferring hexagons.

In his sketch-blog "Krulwich Wonders," National Public Radio science correspondent Robert Krulwich walks readers through the logic of the bees' choice. First and foremost, the bees want to build a structurally tight honeycomb. That means minimizing gaps between cells. If bees constructed their first cell in just any old shape—Krulwich sketches a kidney-shaped blob—the adjoining cell would have to fit neatly, like a jigsaw puzzle, to that shape. That might be theoretically possible, but bees in the wild don't build honeycombs cell by cell, in slow bespoke style. Instead they build many cells rapidly at once, flat-organizational-style.

In fact, if bees want their honeycomb cells to fit neatly together without gaps or overlapping—<u>what mathematicians call "tessellated"</u>—only three regular polygons will accomplish that: squares, equilateral triangles, and hexagons.

So, why hexagons? Varro's conjecture was this: a structure built with hexagons is probably more compact than that built with triangles or squares. In 1999, mathematics professor Thomas Hales published a proof of that very thing. In the argot of math, regular hexagons *do* minimize the perimeter required to enclose units that fill an infinite plane.

Why would bees care about minimizing the perimeter of each cell? (One pictures the kind of bee who'd ask this question: like Brainy Smurf on break from the hive grind.) Krulwich explains: "Compactness matters. The more compact your structure, the less wax you need to construct the honeycomb. Wax is expensive. A bee must consume about eight ounces of honey to produce a single ounce of wax. So if you are watching your wax bill, you want the most compact building plan you can find."

The Language of Bricks

"Dumb as a brick" is a famous insult, but master bricklayers would question the put-down. Perhaps defensively, masonry terminology is vast and technical, infused with surprising whiffs of personality. Consider the following lexicon.

Each side of a brick has a name, according to how it's laid down in a "course," or row of bricks. Picture a brick lying horizontally, with its long narrow side exposed: that's a "stretcher." The same side positioned vertically (for that tall, skinny brick-look) is called a "soldier." Position a brick vertically with its fattest face exposed: that's a <u>"sailor."</u> When that fat face peers outward but lies horizontally, that's a "shiner." The tiniest side of a brick is also rectangle-shaped. If it peeks out from the course, lying on its longer side,

¬ <u>what mathematicians call "tessellated"</u>: Mind, prepare to be blown by patterns of nonlinear geometry and other branches of advanced mathematics. Turn to page 121.

∕ <u>"sailor"</u>: Learn more about French sailors' stripes on page 51.

brick-speak acts like a decoder key to the urban landscape. You start by labeling the brick's faces in every structure you see. Then, almost feverishly, you advance to recognizing the bonds. Every brick wall, cemetery fence, crumbling school, paved-brick alleyway becomes a plainclothes secret, whose names only a few can read.

that's called a "header." When it rests on the rectangle's shorter side, it's a "rowlock." Broken bricks are called "bats" (as in "half-bat" or "three-quarter's bat").

From this concise vocabulary arises a bewildering number of brickwork patterns, all—like knitting instructions—precise in their sequence of headers, shiners, sailors, and what-have-you-else. Among the more colorfully named load-bearing brick patterns (or "bonds"): Raking Monk bond, Double Flemish, English Cross. And this is just the start of a confounding terminology: creasing tiles, quoins, squints, noggins, voussoirs, racking backs, withes . . . the language bricklayers speak is nuanced, compact, elegant, and everywhere. Even a working knowledge of

Curves

Florals

<u>The King of Floral Wallpaper</u>

Who invented that classic of interior design, floral wallpaper? Impossible to say, yet it's very possible to say who popularized it in the industrial era: William Morris.

Born near London in 1834, Morris spent his youth tunneling backward in time: reading archaic tales by <u>Sir Walter Scott</u>, mooning about prehistoric sites at Avebury and Silbury Hill in Wiltshire.

Studying classics at Oxford, he became a lifelong friend of the artist and designer Edward Burne-Jones. Together "Ned" Jones and "Topsy" Morris swooned over Tennyson, Shakespeare, and the throwback aesthetic of their contemporaries, the Pre-Raphaelites. ("Topsy" got his nickname from a character in *Uncle Tom's Cabin*, the inspiration for the saying "to grow like Topsy": rapidly and confusedly. Morris grew this way in his career post-Oxford.)

Like that of any wax-mustachioed hipster, Morris's life involved a mass of contradictions at which he would coolly shrug. Like the Bauhaus after him, Morris admired practical design: one should "have nothing in your houses that you do not know to be useful, or believe to be beautiful." (Unlike the Bauhaus, he revered small-scale production: hardly a precondition of affordability.) A card-carrying socialist, he despised capitalism, though he was the son of a financier and ran his own successful capitalist enterprise, Morris & Co., producing textiles, furnishings, stained glass, and other bougie household treats. (Morris called what he did "ministering to the swinish luxury of the rich.") During his lifetime, the most famous man in wallpaper was best known as a poet, translator—he had a yen for Icelandic sagas—and fantasy writer. (J. R. R. Tolkien named Gandalf after a Morris character.) Morris actually turned down Great Britain's poet-laureate position in 1892; he deemed it too monarchical.

Morris's most iconic wallpapers became—like Eero Saarinen chairs—the covetable home commodity of his day. Interiors of the Gilded Age were densely flowered with Morris designs like Trellis (red poppies snaking through trelliswork, studded by bluebirds), Daisy, Acanthus (swirling dense leaves of same), Pomegranate (lushly split fruits in a spare network of leaves), and Strawberry Thief (eye-poppingly ornate, it takes a few seconds to notice birds eyeing strawberries amid detailed blossoms and vines).

 <u>Sir Walter Scott</u>: A cultural attaché for all things Scottish, Scott stage-managed King George IV's visit to Edinburgh in 1822, a plaid extravaganza of the first order. See page 74.

While his floral patterns covered other goods as well—from throw pillows to furniture to china and beyond—his era's infatuation with wallpaper as the underpinning of a well-dressed room—indeed, a marker of civil society—made the papers his most enduring legacy.

Lecturing on pattern in 1881, Morris remarked, "any decoration is futile . . . when it does not remind you of something beyond itself." Put even more plainly, another Morris pronouncement nails exactly this book's premise: "No pattern should be without some sort of meaning."

Paisley

A World-eating Flower

What form of life is paisley, exactly? The symbol sprang up millennia ago, somewhere between present-day Iran and the Kashmiri region straddling the Indian-Pakistani border. Although it was originally called *būtā* or *boteh*, meaning "flower," in paisley people have seen resemblances to a lotus, a mango, a leech, a yin and yang, a dragon, and a cypress pine. Ancient Babylonians likened it to an uncurling date palm shoot. Providing them with food, wine, wood, <u>paper,</u>

thatch, and string—all of life's necessities—date palms symbolized prosperity and plenty.

Mughal Paisley Princes

Paisley began its life as the privilege of <u>cosseted, powerful men.</u>

Kashmiri shawls sprang up as early as the eleventh century but found their first promoter in Zain-ul-Abidin, who ruled Kashmir from 1459 to 1470 and encouraged weavers from Persia and Central Asia to move to his kingdom. Their next champion was Akbar (reigned 1556–1606), who made the shawls central to the Kashmiri practice of *khil'at*, "robes of honor" ceremonially exchanged in political and religious contexts to establish a clear pecking order. (Being on the receiving end made one submissive and therefore inferior to the giver—not awesome, although scoring the sumptuous textiles made for luxurious compensation.) Shawls given as khil'at were decorated with all sorts of patterns, although some scholars wonder if the paisley motif came to predominate because it resembled *jigha*, a crown insignia jewel used to pin a feather to a courtier's turban. (Gradually the jigha elongated, more and more resembling the feather it anchored. So, yet another reading: paisley is a feather.)

As with so many other luxury goods, there was nothing efficient about making a Kashmiri shawl. Its wool came from a Central Asian species of goat, *capra hircus* in Latin or *shahtoosh* in indigenous terms. These animals wandered into the high Himalayas, where the bitter cold made their

95

- <u>paper:</u> Who knew that blank graph paper contained multiverses? See page 89.
- <u>cosseted, powerful men:</u>
  / When power brokers suit up, they like tattersall dress shirts (page 78), striped ties (page 52), and houndstooth (page 79).

In the village, a sage should go about
Like a bee, which, not harming
Flower, color, or scent,
Flies off with the nectar.

—from *The Dhammapada*, a collection of
aphorisms attributed to the Buddha

underbellies sprout a dense, ultrafine wool. The goats shed this pashmina, as this wool was called, in the summer by rubbing themselves against rocks and bushes; textile workers then literally climbed the Himalayas, collected the fluff by hand, and spun it into thread. (Adding wool from the Tibetan antelope, *chiru*, would skew a shawl farther upmarket. Or you could slum a bit by adding wool combed from domesticated goats.)

Weavers made shawls from the thread using a laborious twill-tapestry technique, which involved weaving the horizontal <u>weft</u> threads around the vertical warp threads only where that color is required in the pattern. (A "color caller" fed the weaver instructions as he progressed.) Individual sections were then carefully and invisibly joined together into a larger shawl. Because it involved so much manual effort, Kashmiri shawls usually sported boteh only at the borders. Making a complex shawl could eat up several years of a Kashmiri weaver's life.

Paisley Storms Europe

Shawls started infiltrating Europe in the late eighteenth century, when Kashmiri princes began including British East India Company officers in their ritual shawl-giving. The English officers sent the shawls home to their sweethearts, who clamored for more. Fresh from conquering Egypt and next sniffing around India, many of Napoleon's officers found themselves stationed near Kashmir and similarly tempted by the shawls. Napoleon's wife Josephine began

stockpiling paisleys, and by the early 1800s, European desire for paisley had intensified into frenzy.

Textile manufacturers noted paisley's ka-ching factor, and the race was on to produce more shawls. Importing finished shawls from Kashmir didn't come close to meeting European demand, so capitalists scrambled to produce their own. Norwich and Edinburgh factories thrummed to life, cranking out worthy imitations, although no amount of tinkering with silk, cotton, and wool blends could compete with the original pashmina wool for softness. A Kashmiri monopoly made the raw material impractical to import, spurring efforts to import the goats instead. Enter William Moorcroft, a British veterinarian who exported fifty shahtoosh goats in 1812, hoping to naturalize them in England. He packed the female goats on one ship, the males on another—a <u>fatal blunder</u>, as it turns out, as the ship carrying the females shipwrecked. A similar experiment in France fared better but also flopped: The surviving goats found the Pyrenees too mild, languishing and then dropping dead. A few dozen goats increased their numbers in Essex in 1828, but they produced a meager quantity of so-so wool. It just wasn't realistic for textile manufacturers to compete with Kashmiri producers on the level of raw materials. So they shifted their focus to gaining other advantages: accelerating production time, lowering manufacturing costs (and retail price), and blitzing consumers with more dazzlingly complex designs.

B <u>weft:</u> Know your warp from your weft and get other textile lingo straight, beginning on page 11.

↗ <u>fatal blunder:</u> "Dazzle-painted" warships in World War I were supposed to throw off the enemy's calculations when aiming at their target. Whether it actually worked or just jazzed up the oceans with a zebra-like fleet is an open question explored on page 65.

A Patterns Arms Race

The next phase of paisley's evolution reads like any technology race, a deadly serious battle for market share wreathed in bobbing exotic boteh. The town of Paisley, Scotland, eclipsed Norwich and Edinburgh in shawl production in the early nineteenth century, thanks to pattern piracy, fast-evolving labor structures, and early adoption of the Jacquard loom. (The latter device automated the manipulation of weft and warp threads necessary to produce complex patterns. It was a total game-changer in textile production.)

Paisley-the-Town's dominance in shawl production explains how the boteh pattern got renamed "paisley" throughout the Western world. (Europeans also used the word "paisley" interchangeably with "shawl"—as in, "Gertrude, your paisley is crooked.") The pattern acquired other nicknames and associations in its migration westward: The French called it at one point "tadpole," the Viennese, "little onion." Quilters gave the pattern their own tender nicknames: "Persian pickles" from the Americans, "Welsh pears" from the Welsh.

Patent wars erupted to protect newfangled designs and the know-how necessary to weave them. Paisley patterns were coveted intellectual property, not unlike computer programs today. Unsurprisingly, legal scuffles only protected European designs; those swiped from the Kashmiris were waved off as fair use.

The Century-long Fashion

Shawls morphed as production technology evolved—so much so, in fact, that paisley stayed fashionable in one form or another for a century. Woven with more primitive looms, early "imitation" shawls were relatively sober: plain or sprigged at the center and patterned only along the borders. As textile technology sped up, richer medallions of paisleys were worked into the shawls' centers, then corners, and finally consumed the entire shawl. You could buy the shawls in many different shapes: modest squares, extra-large handkerchiefs, elongated rectangles, even "plaids" of ten feet by five feet, perfect to accommodate the ever-widening crinoline skirt.

The boteh motif deepened in complexity, too. It started as a naturalistic sprig of flowers that grew denser over the years and later acquired a vase. Gradually the motif abstracted into a teardrop shape, slenderized as its Clark-Kent-like top curl became exaggerated and larger. The flora and fauna bursting from paisleys diversified, too, welcoming Western blooms like carnations, dahlias, and irises as well as snakes, insects, salamanders, and parrots.

Paisleys popped up as outerwear (worn by women and men on open-air carriage rides) and in bridal trousseaux as "kirking shawls" worn by brides in their first outing to church ("kirk") after the wedding. Fresh young things who'd worn paisley as girls matured into mothers, then grandmothers whose female offspring, several generations deep, wore paisley insistently in their own way. When printed (rather than woven) patterned shawls hit the

- **pattern piracy:** Shoe designer Mary Bendalari argued that polka-dot designs should be protected by copyright in a 1936 intellectual property dispute. See page 24.

B **Jacquard loom:** A game-changing technology that fully industrialized weaving and automated the drawloom out of existence. See page 13.

■ **"plaids":** "Tartan" actually refers to what Americans call the plaid pattern. "Plaid" originally meant any wool blanket, whether tartan-patterned or not. See page 72.

● **Clark-Kent-like top curl:** Meet Mister Polka-Dot, a comic-book villain who wielded evil dots as his superpower. See page 32.

☙ **irises:** The most likely model in nature for the abstracted fleur-de-lis. Turn to page 103.

European market in the 1850s and '60s, working-class women could afford "paisleys," too. For a brief, shining moment, all the women in a European household—from the lady down to the scullery maids—draped themselves in paisley.

The spell of paisley finally broke in the 1870s. The Franco-Prussian War of 1870–71 delivered the first blow: The French lost, leaving the country impoverished and depriving the Kashmiri weavers of their biggest export customer. A famine in 1877 decimated the Indian weavers, too. But paisley's popularity ultimately ended thanks to inexorable swings in fashion. In the book *The Paisley Pattern*, authors Valerie Reilly and Frank Ames describe the paisley's demise: "The beginning of the end for the shawl fashion was seen by 1865, when the crinoline skirt began to flatten at the front and bunch up at the back as a prelude to the bustle." As the *Telegraph* dryly noted in 2007, "After a century of adapting the shawl to fashion needs, there was simply no way around the fact that wearing one over your bustle both destroyed the point of having it and made you look like Quasimodo." The century of paisley was over.

Paisley's Half-life

Long after paisleys got pushed to the back of fashionable ladies' closets, the tradition persisted of including a paisley shawl in a bridal trousseau—although, like inscribed baby rings or gorgeously beribboned christening gowns, these shawls generally went unworn. As street-fashion, paisley

reemerged in spurts: around 1904, Norwegian peasant girls and Spanish ladies still favored paisleys as church wear. Opening its doors in 1875, iconic department store Liberty of London first specialized in exotica from the Far East, but they later diversified into their signature "Liberty prints" fabrics for clothing and furniture, many of which include paisley motifs. Toward the end of paisley's heyday, it had also snuck onto smaller, luxurious items for men: smoking jackets, silk handkerchiefs, neckties, and cravats. By wearing a slightly excessive amount of paisley, gay men discreetly signaled their status to one another.

Gay Men, Hippies, and Cowboys

Among the many inexpensive printed cottons produced at the turn of the twentieth century was the bandanna, dotted or paisley-printed against a red or blue background. (The name comes from the Hindi word *bāndhnū*, meaning both "tie-dying" and tying generally.) Cheap, paisley-printed bandannas sprouted around the necks of American cowboys, the sweat-soaked foreheads of farmworkers, and over the noses of wilderness firefighters. Manifest destiny meant America was teeming with pioneers, a market eager to buy rugged work-wear like canvas denim pants and cotton paisley kerchiefs. Printed on a new, rough-and-ready canvas, paisley became a daily comfort of frontier men in the New World.

Paisley also exploded back into vogue in the 1960s. Psychedelically detailed, paisley fed into hippies' fascination with all things Indian. (John Lennon had his Rolls-Royce painted paisley after the Beatles visited India, and the band's embrace of everything Eastern boosted paisley's profile considerably.) Fey, unabashedly lush, rich on its own uncompromising terms, paisley's uncoolness—its original fans were by then great-grandmothers—made the pattern ripe for reappropriation.

Remorselessly, paisley conquered still other social groups. Cruising gay men in 1970s-era San Francisco recalled their nineteenth-century brethren in using paisley as a signal. They invented "handkerchief code," communicating their sexual proclivities by stuffing color-coded paisley bandannas into their back pockets. The rainbow of paisleys matches the rainbow of human desires: lime (likes to eat food off someone's body), mauve (navel sex), apricot (a "chubby chaser"), or the awe of orange (few sexual limits). In the 1980s gang wars, specific colors took on very different meanings for a different demographic: blue-bandanna'd Crips faced off against their rivals, red-bandanna-wearing Bloods. As if to complete the spectrum of oddball paisley-adherents, the Boy Scouts adopted tan-and-blue bandannas to signal troop affiliation, too.

The circle of paisley's irony is now complete. A pattern of exclusive royal privilege in the East becomes the pattern of Western capitalist longing. It trickles down on humbler fabrics to working men, gay men, gang members, and Boy Scouts. It signifies free love and forbidden love, belonging and exclusion—a seemingly impossible range of human experience.

Fleur-de-lis

The First Blockbuster Logo?

Gather round, marketers, for a tale of genius branding: the history of fleur-de-lis. From its misty beginnings, the fleur-de-lis had all the makings of a blockbuster logo. According to the *Traité d'Héraldique* ("Treatise on Heraldry") by Michel Pastoureau, this motif is "common to all epochs, in every civilization . . . It is an essentially graphic theme found on Mesopotamian cylinders, Egyptian bas-reliefs, Mycenaean potteries, Sassanian textiles, Gaulish coins, Mamluk coins, Indonesian clothes, Japanese emblems and Dogon totems."

Start with the obvious question: What is a fleur-de-lis? As with paisley, there's hot debate. While a vocal minority argue it's an iris, seeing in that flower's jowly elegance a more exact resemblance, most scholars maintain it's a lily—*lis* being the lily's name in French.

Lilies have the advantage of being part of Christian symbolism, which no doubt helped the broad embrace of the fleur-de-lis. During the high Middle Ages in Europe, according to Pastoureau, lilies—and fleur-de-lis—were closely associated with Christ himself, stemming from the Song of Solomon 2:1, "I am the rose of Sharon, the lily of the valleys." When the Cult of Mary emerged in the middle of the eleventh century, fleur-de-lis became a Marian symbol of purity as well, a nod to yet another verse in Song of Solomon, 2:2, "like a lily among thorns is my darling among women."

And lilies sprout all over the legend of Clovis, the first Christian king of what would become France, and the figure perhaps initially responsible for the fleur-de-lis's most strongly enduring association: as symbol of all things French. Around 500 C.E. Clovis prayed to his Christian wife Clotilde's God before a key battle with a group of Germanic tribes called the Alamans. When he won, Clovis converted to her faith in thanks and founded France as a Christian nation.

Prior to his conversion, Clovis's coat of arms were either three Muslim crescents (*trois croissants* in French texts, delighting breakfast fans everywhere) or "three toads erect," a demonic or pagan symbol that punches up the drama of Clovis's religious conversion. God supposedly commanded Clovis through an angel to toss his old <u>coat of arms</u> in favor of a new Christian one: the fleur-de-lis.

Interestingly, the legend of Clovis is also adapted as ammunition for the fleur-de-lis-as-iris camp. In one story, after the victorious battle at Tobiacum (Zupich) against the Alamans, Clovis and his army plucked irises from the river

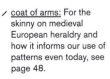

<u>coat of arms:</u> For the skinny on medieval European heraldry and how it informs our use of patterns even today, see page 48.

to adorn their hair—like "flower children" reformed after war, one scholar skeptically remarks. Another story featuring irises: Clovis was searching for a good place to cross a river on the way to his battle with the Alamans. At the opportune moment, a doe leapt across the river, revealing the best place to ford the waters. The army followed suit and made it across. Bending from his horse, Clovis plucked a yellow iris from the riverbank and tucked it into his helmet.

While the lily-versus-iris debate rages onward, other scholars argue the fleur-de-lis is actually a <u>bee</u>. You can gaze cockeyed at a fleur-de-lis and imagine it's a bee pinned, bug-collector-style, with its wings extended to either side. But the bee lobby got really fired up when they found their own Clovis connection: in 1653 when the tomb of Childéric I, Clovis's father, was unearthed near Tournai (in present-day Belgium), three hundred small golden bees tumbled out. Finally, those who don't believe any of the above argue for gadflies, doves, and weapon-heads, all basing their arguments either on a) Just *Look At The Thing* or b) Scholar X Said It Was So.

Vive la France!

When did France adopt the fleur-de-lis as its national symbol? Impossible to say exactly, although historians have jawed plenty on the subject. For centuries, fleur-de-lis effloresced unofficially all over coins, banners, stained-glass windows, scepters in royal portraits—sprouting everywhere, really, like a high-class dandelion. Much as with <u>plaid</u>, the design's origins receded deeper into the past whenever an

extra dollop of ancientness was called for.

Legends have dated the fleur-de-lis all the way back to Clovis, but it wasn't until a good half-millennium later, scholars concur, that the fleur-de-lis became the official royal symbol—about seven or eight King Louis-es in. So many French Louis-es adopted the fleur-de-lis, in fact, that scholars have suggested the motif is a rebus, or cunning pictogram, depicting the phrase "flower of Louis." (And for Clovis fans, it helps to know that "Clovis" is the Latin version of the name "Louis.")

But it was not until Charles V in 1376 that the design of the French royal coat of arms solidified: three gold fleurs-de-lis arranged in a triangle on a field of royal blue. Heraldry scholars dubbed this *azur semé de fleur de lis d'or*.

The fleur-de-lis's meanings continued to morph over the centuries. In religious contexts its three petals made it a nice symbolic stand-in for the Holy Trinity, thus also suggesting the country's saintliness and the French kings' divine right to rule. For occasions when nationalistic brawn was called for, the three petals could stand for faith, wisdom, and chivalry. One historian has argued the three petals represent the medieval social classes of France: those who worked, those who fought, and those who prayed.

Why We Call Frenchies "Frogs"

In 1611, John Guillim's *Display of Heraldrie* described the fleur-de-lis as "three toads erect," *trois crapauds saltant*. Maybe he was confusing it with Clovis's supposed pre-

■ <u>bee:</u> Why are honeycombs always hexagonal in shape? Buzz on over to page 90 for the answer.

■ <u>plaid:</u> Nearly everything you think you know about plaid was actually invented, then furiously believed as true. The full tale begins on page 75.

Nostradamus made centuries earlier: *Les anciens crapauds prendront Sara*—"the ancient toads shall Sara take." "This prophecy of Nostradamus . . . was applied to this event in a somewhat roundabout manner," explains one source. "Sara is Aras backward. By the ancient toads were meant the French, as that name formerly had for its armorial bearings three of those odious reptiles instead of the three fleur-de-lis which it now bears." Nostradamus' toads became fleur-de-lis became Frenchmen called "frogs," collectively known as Monsieur Jean Crapaud. The toad and lily *are* the Walrus!

Felons & Slaves

Fleur-de-lis didn't merely fancy up the aristocracy's stuff. It also marked hardened criminals, slaves, and anyone controlled by the French state.

In the 1844 novel *The Three Musketeers*, by Alexandre Dumas père, the main character, d'Artagnan, faces off against a sexy nemesis, a spy and assassin in the service of Cardinal Richelieu known as Milady de Winter. We find out she's not who she says she is when d'Artagnan glimpses her fleur-de-lis tattoo, revealing she's been imprisoned—and inked—by the French government as a felon.

The practice of *fleurdeliser* (a verb meaning "to mark with the fleur-de-lis") traveled across the waters to French-controlled colonies, including America. Under the Code Noir of 1685, African slaves in these regions were not tattooed but branded with a fleur-de-lis as punishment for their first attempt at escape. It got much worse: On their

Christian coat of arms, or maybe he indeed saw frogginess in the classic fleur-de-lis motif. Clovis's three toads purportedly descended from the three sable frogs featured on his great-grandfather King Pharamond's arms, itself a reference to Pharamond's descent from the river gods. It's-a-frog theorists claim these frogs were adapted in the fleur-de-lis, not abandoned.

But how did heraldic toads get mixed up with an insulting nickname for the French? And why do the French themselves call an everyman *Monsieur Jean Crapaud*, Mr. Johnny Toad? Scholars blame Nostradamus. When Louis XIV's troops seized the city of Aras from the Spaniards, it was broadly interpreted as the fulfilment of a prediction

105

🐸 The toad and lily *are* the Walrus!: The Beatles' fascination with all things Indian fueled paisley's comeback in the 1960s; see page 102.

● tattoo: Five dots arranged as they appear on the five-side of a dice is a popular prison tattoo the world over. See page 38.

I ACCEPT...

THE SPIKE-IRONED COLLARS

AND THE HAMSTRINGING

OF MY RUNAWAY AUDACITY AND

THE FLEUR-DE-LYS FLOWING FROM

THE RED IRON INTO THE FAT OF

MY SHOULDER.

— from *Notebook of a Return to the Native Land*
by Aimé Césaire

second attempt, their hamstrings were severed; on strike three they were killed.

Fleur-de-lis still figure in the flags for American cities established by the French: St. Louis, Louisville, Detroit, and New Orleans among others. Fleur-de-lis tattoos flourished in a more self-determined way among those displaced by Hurricane Katrina who, stamped the memory of their city, and their hopes for renewal, on their flesh. "If you get tattooed, it's gonna last forever," Randy Muller of Eye Candy Tattoos in New Orleans told the *Journal of Jefferson Parish* in 2008. "Your house can burn down, your house can get flooded. Nobody's gonna take your tattoos. It's the only thing you'll ever buy that you'll take with you until you die."

Say It With (Patterned) Flowers

Kanga

Much like the messages encoded in Asante <u>kente cloth</u>, flowery textiles communicate specific meanings in cultures around the world. Messages semaphore silently from woman to woman, like wafting scents detectable only to the female nose.

Take the cotton rectangular *kanga* cloth of Kenya and East Africa, also called *leso*, *kikoy*, or *pagne*. Each kanga expresses a specific motto in a floral or vegetal motif framed in a border. The text version of the saying appears along the bottom border, in the same place a legend on an oil painting might go. Because kangas are worn wrapped around the body, others only glimpse bits of the pattern and rarely see the text part: a form of coyness suited to the Swahili ideal of a quiet, forbearing woman. But kanga-mistresses know their patterns cold, recognizing and parsing them rapidly.

Kanga commentary can be salty, pointed, musing, or philosophical. It runs to <u>slut-shaming</u> ("You can visit all the butchers, but the meat is the same"), lay-off-my-man warnings ("You are crossing my boundary, watch out for my date tree"), chiding gossips ("How did you know this if you didn't go behind my back?"), as well as less barbed observations ("Education is an ocean: that is, it has no end") and pragmatic life lessons ("The person who laughs at another's scar hasn't been wounded yet").

Kanga are mostly intended as messages between women, No Boys Allowed. But occasionally men catch their drift. One scholar relates a story of a recently divorced man who quickly began seeing a new woman. The man noticed how

/ <u>kente cloth:</u> Bold, stripe-heavy patterns originating with the Asante and Ewe peoples of Ghana. Each kente pattern encodes a well-known saying. See page 63.

● <u>slut-shaming:</u> In the long century between the 1590s and the 1720s, "patching" was all the rage among fashionable ladies—much to the chagrin of various prudes. See page 41.

his new woman often wore kanga cloths bedecked with wild spiders, an exceedingly subtle message that penetrated when one day he remembered the proverb: "What one does to *cendaa* (a small harmless spider), one does not do to *bokohulu* (a large spider considered dangerous)." Translation, intuited by this sensitive gent and confirmed by the woman in question: Don't mistreat me as you did your first wife.

Lamba Hoany

Women in Madagascar wear cotton *lamba hoany* cloths, whose proverbs bridge the island's eighteen ethnic groups and dialects. Lamba hoany are both gorgeous and all-purpose, used as aprons, baby-carriers, shawls, and sarongs suitable for messy work, even formally as funeral attire. They resemble their East African cousin kanga in looks—deeply saturated colors, floral-heavy in pattern, often with text printed right onto the cloth—but lamba hoany proverbs draw on a different collection of mottos. For instance: "A rolling stone never stops until it reaches the bottom," referring to an angry person's tendency to run off disastrously at the mouth. If you're in a situation where you're unsure what to do next, don the lamba hoany bemoaning the stepchild's dilemma: "If he doesn't wash his hands, he's called dirty. If he does, he's wasting the water." On self-sacrifice and the Sisyphean nature of cleaning—two topics women tend to know way too much about—there's this lamba hoany proverb: "Cleansing others, but wasting away in the process, like soap." Or this world-weary observation: "Don't be so

much in love that you can't see when the rain is coming."

Other lamba hoany proverbs wax sunny and philosophical. "Something that is full will not slosh around," remarks one saying, meaning a life that's busy and diverse in activities will be contained, under control. Another, perhaps the most popular of Malagasy sayings, presents life as a thrillingly open road: "Everybody goes, everybody searches."

Oya

A Turkish woman's headscarf is sometimes edged with 3-D flower embroidery, called *oya*. What these decorations signaled until the early twentieth century was discernible only to other traditional Turkish women—much like Shakespearean audiences understood the symbolic meanings of plants Ophelia distributes in her "crazy flowers" speech in *Hamlet*.

While mustaschioed groomsmen beamed down on a blushing Turkish bride, her "sea-holly" oya would prick her mother-in-law's eye with a more pointed request: Don't sting me like a thorn. Lacing a woman's headscarf with oya chile peppers announced silently that, right then, things between husband and wife were fractious and "hot"— much like daisies in Shakespearean times communicated faithlessness and dissembling. Oya pansies invited other women to commiserate silently on a roving husband.

You could layer meanings in your oya designs as well. Edging any oya flower in green reflected satisfaction in marriage, while a yellow border signaled unhappiness or annoyance.

Oya could speak eloquently in gift-exchanges, too. Say a mother-in-law received a scarf lined with a well-spaced border of embroidered meadow flowers. Translation: My marriage to your son is going swimmingly, thanks.

Hiding in Plain Sight

Camouflage's Contradictions

Camouflage is a pattern of paradox. Throughout its history camo hasn't only, or even primarily, been concerned with hiding. It's also been about *being seen*: confusing the eye, subverting reality, asserting both individuality and group identities. Camouflage is a pattern, a collection of conflicting verbs, and a surprisingly multivalent worldview.

The term "camouflage" has a layered etymology that betrays the kind of everyday magic militaries hoped it would provide them. Dating to sixteenth-century France, a *camouflet* was a <u>practical joke</u> that involved "lighting the tip of a hollow paper cone, then holding the opposite smoldering end under [a] sleeper's nose. The stupefied sleeper would spring to his feet as soon as a noseful of smoke was inhaled." Camouflet later referred to a "small but lethal powder charge by which a tunneling enemy troop could be entrapped beneath the ground." But camouflage also stems from the French verb *camoufler*, to make oneself up for the stage.

The improbable history of military camouflage united a cast of thousands in perhaps *the* most democratic visual literacy course ever taught. With hundreds of patterns and dozens of conflicting uses—by everyone from 1920s flappers to Public Enemy to proud redneck prom queens—camouflage embodies the modern era's cultural wars as much as its military conflicts.

Animals, Artists, & Optics

Camouflage arose from a perfect intellectual storm in the early twentieth century; its underlying concepts were floating in the water of several disciplines at once.

British zoologist Sir Edward Poulton wrote the first book on camouflage in 1890. An ardent Darwinist before it was fashionable, Poulton saw animal self-concealment by

∕ <u>practical joke:</u> For a laugh, ask the new guy working on your construction site to fetch you "striped paint." See page 69.

The temple bell stops but I still hear the sound coming out of the flowers.

—Matsuo Bashō, seventeenth-century Japanese poet

mimicry as proof of natural selection. Whether it means masquerading as a twig, a wood ant (when actually a rove beetle), or a poisonous valentine puffer fish (when actually harmless), *mimicry* is a <u>bluffer's gift</u> used by predators and prey alike. Later generations of zoologists, chief among them another Brit, Hugh Cott, in 1940, affirmed and expanded on these ideas.

In 1896, American painter and naturalist Abbott Thayer published an essay, "The Law Which Underlies Protective Coloration," in an academic journal for ornithologists. In it he expounded on two key ideas in camouflage: countershading and disruptive coloration. *Countershading* explains why so many animals have a lighter underbelly shading into a darker top. This visual effect cancels out shadowing from overhead sun, rendering the animal flat and insubstantial-looking. *Disruptive coloration* refers to any irregular patterning on an animal's skin that disrupts its contours, making it more difficult to perceive at a distance.

Thayer attracted both popular interest and pungent criticism for his theories on camouflage. Later in life, he wrote with increasing zeal in his own defense, but he also succumbed to panic attacks and bipolar disorder.

Other visual artists were enamored of advances in optics like <u>Gestalt theory</u>, the way our brains perceive discrete objects, even amid lots of visual hubbub. Pointillists like Georges Seurat in the late nineteenth century broke their images into tiny dots, while Cubists and Vorticists of the early twentieth century tried to show multiple perspectives of a 3-D object on a flat canvas.

Whether these artistic experiments influenced military camouflage or vice versa is unclear, but artists liked to think they were first. Seeing a camouflaged cannon rolling through Paris during World War I, Pablo Picasso exclaimed: *"C'est nous qui avons fait ça!"* ("We created that!"). Later he assumed a breezy expertise on how disruptive coloration works: "If they only want to make an army invisible at a distance," he told poet Jean Cocteau, "they have only to dress their men as harlequins."

<u>The Precursors to Military Camo</u>

An early master of camouflage tactics—if not the pattern proper—were Jamaican Maroons, <u>African slaves</u> who forced their British colonists to give them independent lands in the eighteenth century. Led by Nanny, one of Jamaica's few female national heroes, the Maroons used camouflage to foil the British at every turn: cladding themselves in foliage, communicating via birdcalls, even disguising their trail with lemon-scented leaves to confuse British bloodhounds.

European armies wore bright uniforms until the mid-eighteenth century, when the invention of rifles—a more accurate weapon than muskets—allowed sharpshooters to pick off their enemies. Austrian *Jägers* (literally "hunters") started dressing for this specialized job in light gray, while the British 95th Rifle Regiment wore dun-green.

"Khaki" entered the lexicon in the mid-nineteenth century, when soldiers in the British Indian Army, dressed in hot-weather white, began to dye their duds with tea and

---

■ <u>bluffer's gift</u>: The history of tartan is still full of bullshit artists. See pages 75 and 76.

B <u>Gestalt theory</u>: See page 17.

❤ <u>African slaves</u>: In French-controlled colonies, slaves got branded with a fleur-de-lis after their first escape attempt. See page 105.

curry. Named for Urdu and Persian words for dust, khaki was less visible than white and lots more practical. Militaries adopted drab uniforms broadly around the world at the turn of the twentieth century.

Camouflage in World War I

"The birth of modern camouflage was a direct consequence of the invention of the airplane," wrote Tim Newark in his 2007 book *Camouflage*. Worried about aerial reconnaissance, militaries first used camouflage to hide equipment and locations, not people. (Aerial attack emerged as a threat later.)

The French were first to organize camouflage units,

known as *camoufleurs*, around 1914. Early camo tactics were basic: hand-painting a splotchy pattern on tanks, trucks, and cannons in whatever colors matched the battleground landscape. Camoufleurs also tossed netting laced with raffia ties over valuable buildings to imitate foliage, and taught troops ways to reduce their aerial visibility: smoothing over truck tracks and cannon blast marks, parking tanks under trees to reduce telltale shadows, and so forth.

Camo grew increasingly baroque as World War I progressed. Battalions of howitzers might be shrouded in a tarp painted to resemble fake farmland. Munitions factories stamped out thousands of decoy human heads, to be poked provocatively above a trench line, attracting enemy fire that betrayed his location. A mania for false trees as observation posts swept the regiments. An actual tree in a battlefield would be felled in the wee hours, and a hollowed-out replica erected in its place (with a soldier smuggled inside it). This ploy got Charlie Chaplin into hot water in a scene from his 1918 war film *Shoulder Arms*. His snooping proximity to a German campfire takes a hair-raising turn when the Jerries run out of firewood and come at Charlie a-choppin'.

Allies also cloaked their warships in "dazzle paint," incongruously jazzy, zebra-like stripes. As its chief military advocate described it, dazzle wasn't at all aimed at hiding a warship but instead was intended to "break up her form [to] thus confuse a submarine officer as to the course on which she was heading."

Despite this mania for camouflaging equipment, most soldiers wore solid drab uniforms in World War I. Camouflage first crept onto the ranks as sharpshooter garb, conveying elite status in much the way drab originally did.

The Germans decorated their *Stahlhelm* (steel helmets) in a disruptive pattern; trench-assaulting storm troopers wore these starting in 1916. "Ghillie suits" worn by British snipers turned them into walking shrubs. (The name stems from a Gaelic term for landowners' servants who hid in wait to snag poachers.) Disruptively patterned ghillie bodysuits came with matching balaclavas and three-fingered mittens (to accommodate the trigger finger); soldiers stuck greenery into the fabric to complete the ruse. The look perfectly combined a Klansman-like severity with a certain hangdog awareness of how ridiculous one looked. Still: hot, inconvenient, and mockable as they were, a good ghillie suit worked.

World War II

The increasing threat of aerial attacks meant that even doubters turned to camouflage in the ramp-up to World War II. With the notable exception of dazzle, all the camo-tactics of World War I were expanded, including training. Overenthusiastic civilians and troops often produced terrible camouflage—"like a Macgregor tartan at a Brixton funeral," as one scholar puts it—suggesting a pressing need for education.

A shower of booklets, posters, and flyers explained what effective camouflage looked like, using every ploy to grab their audience's attention. Surrealist painter (and British camoufleur) Roland Penrose spiced up his training slideshow with a naked image of his wife Lee Miller, smeared in camo paint and tangled in netting. A U.S. Army training manual featured pinup girl Chili Williams in a camo-themed spread from *Life* magazine.

Camouflage patterns also spread more broadly to uniforms during World War II, bringing their distinctive varieties into sharper focus. Never just a single pattern, "camouflage" expanded to a category encompassing hundreds of designs. Each country created its own pattern with versions for different fighting conditions (forest, snow, desert, jungle). Each pattern was tinkered with as war technologies advanced.

Camouflage played a key role in two Allied wins: El Alamein in 1942 and D-Day in 1944.

At the Second Battle of El Alamein, the Allies prevented German commander Erwin Rommel from driving through

113

/ "dazzle paint": See page 65.

/ zebra-like: See page 66.

■ Macgregor tartan: Dive into the weirdness of plaid starting on page 72.

Egypt to seize Mideast oil reserves and the Suez Canal. To achieve this, they had to make Rommel believe an attack was brewing to the south of the Alamein line. So the Allies staged a fake supply buildup over a period of weeks south of El Alamein, replete with inflatable tanks, phony artillery flashing, and a false extension of an existing water pipeline southward. British camoufleur and stage magician Jasper Maskelyne was the mastermind of El Alamein's most audacious feat: hiding the entire Suez Canal from aerial view with a system of mirrors attached to massive searchlights, which projected rotating light beams into the night sky to thwart enemy pilots. In October 1942 the Allies attacked to the north, catching the Wehrmacht unawares and turning the tide to an eventual Allied victory.

The Allies used similar camo tactics to achieve victory on D-Day. First they leaked a credible but fake war plan to the Germans. In keeping with the fake plan, Allied troops seemed to be amassing in Scotland and Kent to attack Norway—while actually concentrating forces aimed at Normandy. Movie studios helped construct a head-spinning number of false oil storage tanks, landing jetties, and inflatable tanks, while creating blinds to cover real troop buildup. The ruse continued after landing in France with the 603rd Engineer Camouflage Battalion of the U.S. Army. This "Ghost Army" took the place of a U.S. battalion actually marching stealthily to Normandy. The Ghost Army had recruited many young artists as camoufleurs, including some bound for later fame: artist Ellsworth Kelly, fashion designer Bill Blass, set designer and actor George Diestel, and Ed Haas (co-creator of *The Munsters*).

Shape-shifting Camo Patterns

After World War II ended, many colonial empires disintegrated. Who chose to wear which camo pattern revealed old colonial relationships, newly shifting alliances, and ironic twists of surplus trade. Massive overruns of British Disruptive Pattern Material (DPM) were sold to the Iraqis mid-century, necessitating a redesign in the first Gulf War when Brits and Iraqis faced off in identical gear. A similar surplus put U.S. "frog camouflage" onto French Indochine soldiers, requiring the United States to switch to "Tigerstripe" for the Vietnam War.

U.S. Army patterns keep evolving: M81 Woodland in 1965 became US Woodland in 1981; "Chocolate chip" appeared in 1992 for the first Iraq War, evolving in 2001 to MARPAT, a digitally pixelated pattern.

Nazi-era camouflage offers an example of how a pattern's provenance can uncomfortably resonate. Patterns like *Splittermuster* ("splinter"), *Erbsenmuster* ("pea"), *Eichenlaubmuster* ("oak leaf"), and *Platanenmuster* ("plane tree") were altered or discontinued after World War II. (The hard-headed Swiss continued wearing *Leibermuster*, an abstracted Nazi pattern, with only minor revisions until 1993.) Military lore has it that Arab troops fighting the Israelis in the 1970s pointedly wore Nazi-era patterns until international backlash caused them to rethink their strategy. Clandestine Neo-Nazi markets keep these patterns in active trade today.

Sometimes, though, an enemy's design was too good *not* to use. As U.S. troops invaded Grenada in 1983 wearing Nazi-influenced "Fritz" helmets, a veteran of World War II

/ "Tigerstripe": What symbolic meanings lurk behind the tiger's stripes? See page 54.

■ Arab troops: An abbreviated history of the Palestinian kaffiyeh pattern starts on page 84.

remarked about his fellow soldiers: "I used to shoot at guys who looked like that."

Camo continues to advance for future conflicts. Innovations include "stealth ponchos" concealing body heat, vinyl-adhesive photos to hide landmarks, and fabrics embedded with fiber optics that sense and dynamically match their surroundings. Camo designer Guy Cramer claims to be perfecting technology that bends the light spectrum to make objects entirely disappear.

Beyond the Battlefield

The Great Wars yielded many pop-culture riffs on camouflage, although few wearable ones. Camo-themed amusement rides, camo board games, even decoy cows littered civilian culture with camo. Beauty columnists rushed to adapt camo know-how: A 1919 newspaper article trumpeted "Camouflage for Fat Figures and Faulty Faces." The idea of camouflage became a catchall term for how the world is not always as it seems.

Artists saw other ideas embedded within camo: the obliteration of self in society, protest against totalitarianism, the alienation of mass media.

Part of a series, Andy Warhol's *Camouflage Self-Portrait* in 1986 shows his face in a Polaroid, silk-screened over with garishly colored U.S. Woodland camo. Here is camo as the distorting thicket of celebrity. Other artists who used recognizable military patterns include Pop artist Alain Jacquet, Marilyn Lysohir, David Bower, and Adelle Lutz

(whose works include the sculpture *His/Hers Combat Lawn Furniture* and camo-costumes for David Byrne's 1986 film *True Stories*).

Other artists skipped the patterns and simply merged themselves into landscapes. Holger Trülzsch photographed 1970s fashion model Vera Lehndorff (aka "Veruschka") melting into African veldts, industrial wastelands, and merry-go-rounds, an inversion of fashion's usually egocentric images. Chinese dissident Liu Bolin's works comment on how the individual gets steamrolled by totalitarianism and capitalism. Via painstaking body-painting, Bolin has rendered himself a nearly invisible shimmer in front of China's Great Wall and the Temple of Heaven in Beijing, as well as the "Bird's Nest" stadium constructed for the Beijing Olympics. Dutch artist Desiree Palmen's use of camouflage merges her own figure into harmless-looking urban scenes: a figure melting into a park bench, subway seats, rain-slicked pavement. She registers only as a slight disturbance in the air, as if souls took up physical space.

Camo for Fashion and Sport

Camouflage clothing lay dormant until the 1960s, when postcolonial revolts, paramilitary movements, and sympathetic youth started wearing the patterns. It was a military fabric for squares, designed to deceive, but also primed for irony. Worn by once-trim, now shaggy veterans in the Vietnam Veterans Against the War organization, the inversion was beautifully complete: Camo now symbolized an aggressive push for peace.

Today camo penetrates all levels of fashion. Musicians wear camouflage to support revolution of various kinds: from black power (Public Enemy) to Sinn Féin and African rights (U2 and Bono). American designer Stephen Sprouse reproduced Warhol's pop-camo in his 1987 collection, a tradition continued by Jean Paul Gaultier, Prabal Gurung, and Patrik Ervell. Camo thus crossed over into the female, suggesting wit and tough beauty.

Hunters usually don't share politics with designers, feminists, or rappers—but they do share a love of camo. Hunters have developed their own camo patterns, distancing themselves visually from the military. The 1970s saw the invention by Jim Crumley of the Trebark pattern, which spawned many imitators including the popular Mossy Oak pattern. (When the Panamanian general Manuel Noriega was finally captured wearing Trebark, Crumley considered featuring him in an ad campaign with the slogan, "No wonder it took so long to capture him," but ultimately decided it was in poor taste.)

Camouflage formalwear brings high and low fashion into collision; sites like CamoFormal.com and ATouchof Camo.com sell it briskly. Girls wearing camouflage formalwear signal a range of conflicting messages: *I like to shoot; I'm proud of my hunting heritage; I can't be pigeonholed; screw all this formality; look at me, in my gown designed to hide.*

Camouflage's final trick may be how thoroughly—indeed, invisibly—it pervades our modern world. Oscar Wilde once observed, "It is only shallow people who do not judge by appearances. The true mystery of the world is the visible, not the invisible." Camouflage's plain face masks a very modern awareness: that the visible world is constructed, contingent, shaped in ways we can barely guess at.

Hunters usually don't share politics with designers: Another unlikely alliance of admirers has collected around paisley. See page 102.

Camouflage is all the rage.
Ladies in their fight with age—
Soldiers in their fight with foes—
Demagogues who mask and pose
In the guise of statesmen—girls
Black of eyes with golden curls—
Politicians, votes in mind,
Smiling, affable and kind,
All use camouflage to-day.
As you go upon your way,
Walk with caution, move with care;
Camouflage is everywhere!

**—World War I-era poem
by Ella Wheeler Wilcox**

Off

the

Pattern
as
Puzzle

Pattern Poetry

Pattern Poetry: Guide to an Unknown Literature (1987) by Dick Higgins studies pattern writ visible, literally. (Higgins was a poet of the Fluxus movement, a freewheeling experimental art collective ascendent in the 1960s.) A quick perusal spins the reader past innumerable poems shaped like crosses or urns; many love-knots (poetry fashioned in an endless knot, the lines of which can be read in any order); language mazes and at least one acrostic gravestone; Hebrew micrography (texts pulled from biblical law and shaped into griffins, dragons, or geometrical webs); and a Spanish-language journal, *El Piston*, devoted to pattern poetry

from the 1860s. More exotic felicities include Arabic kufic inscriptions, an ornamental calligraphy style in which letters are distorted with squared edges to fill a shape; and Indian *citrakāvyas* (poems shaped like wheels, lotuses, swords, necklaces, or "the path of falling urination of a cow").

Pattern Poetry also includes related visual-literary arts, from rebuses (a kind of Charades-on-Paper, in which pictograms are substituted for words in the text) to musical-score analogues, like Haydn's bull's-eye-shaped score *Das erste Gebot* (actually playable) or *Die Katzensymphonie* by Moritz von Schwind, musical staff-paper romping with black-silhouette cats (not at all playable, but primed for viral-Interwebs glory).

A particularly virtuosic form of pattern poetry is Chinese *hui-wen*, palindromic verses whose shape on the page often reflects its subject—for instance, a peach-shaped, palindromic poem about *pantao*, a mythical fruit growing in Taoist paradise. The earliest recorded hui-wen plays a pivotal role in the fourth century B.C.E. story of high-ranking official Dou Tau and his wife Su Hui. Dou Tau took a concubine, Zhao Yangtai, which predictably pissed off his jealous wife. To exact her revenge, Su Hui had her husband's lover beaten and humiliated. Dou Tau wasn't overly chuffed by his wife's brutality, but then again his concubine behaved badly, too, slandering his wife in a stream of backhanded compliments. When Dou Tau accepted a post in a distant province, he invited his wife Su Hui to accompany him, but she refused out of spite. So along Lady Concubine came instead.

⟋ at least one acrostic gravestone: New patterns-in-cemeteries trend: QR codes on headstones that tell the deceased's life story. See page 62.

⌐ Arabic kufic inscriptions: Skip ahead to page 122.

● *Die Katzensymphonie* by Moritz von Schwind: An accidental companion piece to that other toe-tapper, "Pussy's Polka (Composed by Kitty)." For the entwined crazes for polka music and polka dots, turn to page 23.

⟋ jealous wife: Su Hui might have qualified as a "white tiger," a chastisement in Chinese for a quarrelsome woman. For more lore on tigers and their stripes, turn to page 54.

Heartsick at how she had left things with her husband, Su Hui composed an extraordinary palindrome verse to him by way of apology. Now known as the Xuanji Diagram, this hui-wen was a tour de force—and it's not written, it's *embroidered*: more than two hundred poems packed into eight square inches of lustrous silk, the lines making beautiful sense no matter in which order they are read. She sent it by messenger to her husband, who promptly banished his concubine and fetched Su Hui to reunite with him. So ornate was this hui-wen that subsequent readers often fail to grasp the poem's full sense. Su Hui laughed off her contemporaries' confusion with the poem, remarking: "As it lingers aimlessly, twisting and turning, it takes on a pattern of its own. No one but my beloved can be sure of comprehending it." If so inclined, one can also render Dou Tau and Su Hui's Happily-Ever-After-Moment palindromically: "Are we not drawn onward, we few, drawn onward to new era?"

Islamic Patterning

Erasure is manifest everywhere in Islamic patterning. The patterns' creators are stubbornly anonymous. Per Koranic law, resemblances to the actual world are smoothed into abstraction. Solid objects covered in Islamic patterns appear to melt into floating canvases for ideas. Every Islamic pattern is centerless yet potentially infinite, like Allah's ubiquity.

Islamic patterns sprang from the Arab world's pioneering advances in geometry. Each pattern starts with a grid that gets consumed by voracious decoration. Indeed, the objective of the game seems to be inventing a pattern-making process that makes the supporting grid vanish, while also expressing Allah's holiness in mathematical principles. A classic starting point for the Islamic craftsman is to draw one circle, then six interlocking circles: a visual echo of the Koranic six days of creation. By connecting the interstices of these circles, other shapes emerge with their own points of intersection. More connect-the-dots play between those shapes builds intricate patterns that gradually fill the plane.

A particular Islamic favorite is a pattern combining hexagons with six-pointed stars: What Jews and Christians call the Star of David, Muslims call the Seal of Solomon. Other oft-repeated patterns and shapes earned their own names and stories. Consider a pattern of diagonal squares overlaid on each other so they make eight-point stars. Half of the squares appear to expand, the other half to contract, thus explaining this pattern's name, "The Breath of the Compassionate." It's a nod to the teachings of the Great Master Ibn al-'Arabī, who expounds the Divine Breath as the basis for creation, unlocking the possibilities in nature's four elements. Another well-known pattern starts with a grid of decagons separated by bow-tie shapes. Imagine you trace stars starting at the midpoints of each decagon's edge until you've obliterated the bow ties. The resulting pattern is what Persians call *Umm al-Girih*, the "mother of all patterns" (*girih* means "knots") and the first generation of a whole family of useful shapes.

Islamic patterns also often play with numbers, whose mathematical properties informed their symbolism. For instance, twelve is the first *abundant* number, a number whose factors sum to more than itself (1+2+3+4+6=16). Like the abundance of Allah's creation, twelve-fold patterns abound across the Muslim world.

Arabic kufic calligraphy renders words into patterns in a squared black script. Kufic experts can recognize whole phrases embedded in geometric patterns, illegible to ordinary Arabic speakers, like secret holy QR codes.

In Islamic patterning, subverting grids invites transcendence. Every surface in the physical world is perforated, to let the unseen and eternal poke through.

Left-Brained Pattern Bonanza!

Knots

Patterns in knots can be merely pretty, but they can also communicate hard facts and figures.

Some minor examples: On the Ryukyu Islands, a chain of tiny islands stretching from Japan to Taiwan, workmen still braid strands of straw or reeds with knotted fringes to record wages they've earned. Until the twentieth century German millers and bakers could glance at the knot closing a bag of milled grain and know instantly what kind of flour it contained and how much the bag weighed.

But the most ambitious example is *khipu*, a complex system of knotted cords used by the Inca to record tribute payments, inventories, censuses, calendars, even laws,

∕ secret holy QR codes: Actually, QR codes that touch on the afterlife are increasingly a global fad. See page 62.

■ a bag of milled grain: A Persian fable involving a chessboard explains the "wheat problem," illustrating the principle of geometric progression. See page 81.

contracts and historical events. Each khipu starts with a horizontal thread, like a necklace, from which a few or hundreds of strings were hung vertically like pendants. In *Textiles: The Whole Story*, scholar Beverly Gordon explains how khipu accommodated all that complexity: "Each pendant . . . contained sequences of knots that might be tied in a number of different ways: some were tied right over left, and others left over right; some were looser than others; some were single and others double. Spaces between the knots, and cord color and composition also varied, and there might be added-in tufts of fiber or ornamental 'knobs.'" Experts estimate that more than fifteen hundred informational "bits" can be stored with khipu—more units than one would need to read a newspaper in a pictographic language like Chinese.

Math and Science Patterns

How many types of wallpaper patterns exist? If you're querying mathematicians, not interior decorators, the answer is surprisingly crisp: seventeen. That is to say, if you take a figure through every possible combination of rotation and reflection on a flat plane, you'll wind up with seventeen different pattern types—no more, no less. Mathematicians call these the "plane groups" or, more whimsically, "wallpaper groups."

How many regular polygons can fill a flat plane all by themselves, with no gaps and no overlaps? Three: equilateral triangles, squares, and regular hexagons. In other words, only three-, four-, or six-sided regular polygons can *tessellate* a plane without assistance from other shapes. Five-sided regular polygons—or pentagons—won't work by themselves, but if you pair them with the Big Polygonal Three, you can mix and match and fill planes in exactly twenty-five different patterns. If you allow yourself to use any shape, not just regular polygons, you can tile a plane in zillions of interesting ways: Math-loving illustrator M. C. Escher found quite a few, as in his woodcut *Sky and Water I*, in which a pattern of flying geese tiles a plane, while also slowly morphing into fish.

Once patterns bust off the flat surface and into three dimensions, all kinds of spooky symmetrical patterns come to the fore. *Radial* symmetries describe patterned growth forming a sphere; snowflakes, dandelion fluff, sea urchins, dividing cells, and citrus fruits all grow radially. Radial symmetry also describes how most plant stalks grow: in an ever-expanding circle around a long polar axis. "Because plants are usually fixed and nonmotile they tend to be radial," writes David Wade in his book *Symmetry: The Ordering Principle*, "whereas the majority of animals move of their own volition and as a result are *bi-lateral* or, more accurately, *dorsiventral*." Most animals' bodies are symmetrical along a central line, and that line usually points in the direction we move in. (Picture any four- or more-legged animal; its spine is the central line pointing the way forward.)

Another odd symmetry trait humans have in common with other organisms is "handedness." (Biologists call this phenomenon *enantiomorphy*, while chemists favor the term *chirality*.) Handedness manifests itself in ways both predictable (crabs favoring one claw over another) and

123

● wallpaper patterns: Meet arguably the most famous wallpaper designer ever, William Morris, on page 94.

■ *tessellate*: Filling a flat plane efficiently with zero gaps is surprisingly important to bees. To understand why, turn to page 90.

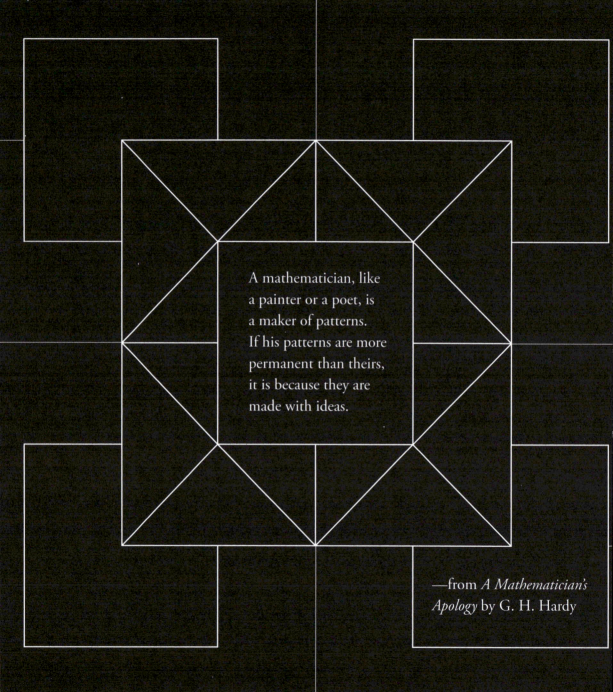

A mathematician, like
a painter or a poet, is
a maker of patterns.
If his patterns are more
permanent than theirs,
it is because they are
made with ideas.

—from *A Mathematician's
Apology* by G. H. Hardy

unpredictable: Twisting vines, seashells, animal horns, and DNA helixes have to choose in which direction, left or right, they'll spin. (Mostly, nature is a righty.) Even molecules display handedness: lemon and orange molecules feature the exact same pattern of elements, just mirror-reversed in structure. Ditto spearmint and caraway. Even sweet and bitter tastes are mirror-obverses of each other, different only in their handedness.

Crystallographers get even more hardcore. Crystalline structures (like diamonds) are almost unnervingly symmetrical, exactly patterned down to the molecular level. Crystallographers have identified exactly fourteen different Bravais lattice structures: regularly repeating patterns of molecules that allow a crystal's structure to repeat infinitely in three spatial dimensions.

Early crystallographers stayed busy simply classifying crystals into groups with similar symmetries. They counted 32 distinct crystal classes and 230 different space-groups. Then in the 1980s a new kingpin rolled into town, Israeli scientist Dan Shechtman. The material he discovered, his namesake Shechtmanite, rocked the crystallography scene. Semiperiodic in structure, it shredded prior laws of crystallography and defined a brand-new class of quasicrystals: materials halfway between unpatterned glass and perfectly patterned diamonds.

Mathematicians studying curvature and flow look at patterns as they evolve in four dimensions, that is space *and* time: curling plumes of smoke, buoys bobbing in water. (Slack-jawed, these guys could gaze at these flow patterns, called *Karman vortices*, for hours.) It might just look like a dripping faucet to you, but in its periodicity mathematicians see the work of *strange attractors*, complex nonlinear shapes that reveal invisible but unmistakable pattern in otherwise chaotic-looking phenomena. "One of the most famous of these is the Lorenz attractor," writes David Wade in *Symmetry: The Ordering Principle*, "which forms the basis of chaotic models in weather prediction (including Ice-Ages)." Another concept of chaos-theory geometries, the Feigenbaum number, "predicts the complex, period-doubling values across a whole range of non-linear phenomena, including turbulence . . . It is, in short, a universal constant like pi or phi, and has a similar symmetrical potency." This is uncanny pattern in nature, existing in both space and time, at scales large and miniscule, explaining the quicksilver movement of quarks to fronts of weather.

Fractals

In his seminal 1982 book *The Fractal Geometry of Nature*, Benoît Mandelbrot explains how geometry got its reputation as bloodless and abstract: because the icily perfect cubes it describes resemble not at all the shaggy actual shapes found in nature. "Clouds are not spheres, mountains are not cones, coastlines are not circles, and bark is not smooth . . . Nature exhibits not simply a higher degree but an altogether different level of complexity."

To understand fractals—the term comes from the Latin *fractus*, meaning "broken"—think first of a head of cauliflower. If you break off one floret, that part exactly resembles the whole head. Tear off a sprig of that floret, and that tinier piece also resembles the whole. And so on and so on, ripping your <u>infinite cauliflower</u> to shreds. Mathematicians would say the cauliflower's pattern of growth exhibits "self-similarity," a chief feature of fractals.

Fractal-fascination traces back to 1877 when a German mathematician, Georg Cantor, started a recursive process that eventually drove him mad. He took a straight line, erased the middle third of it, then performed the same process on the resulting two lines, then again on the resulting four lines, and so on. It occurred to him that the collection of lines was infinite, but each line contained an infinite number of points. His line-erasing game had somehow yielded a number set larger than infinity. Small wonder that this disturbing branch of math was labeled "pathological curves" and shunned for decades.

It was reopened, in large part, by Benoît Mandelbrot, a Lithuanian Jew born in Poland whose peripatetic career took him to IBM's research department in Upstate New York. There he pursued a mathematics that could finally account for the rough "pathological curves" prevalent everywhere in nature. Early in his career he wrestled with what seemed like a simple question: How long is the coast of Britain? The answer, as it turns out, changes depending on how closely you look. Zoom out and measuring the smoothed-out coast appears straightforward. Hone in on the jagged details, however, and you find there's literally more coast to measure. "Here is a question, a staple of grade-school geometry, that if you think about it, is impossible," Mandelbrot told the *New York Times* shortly before his death in 2010. "The length of the coastline, in a sense, is infinite."

Taking advantage of IBM's souped-up computing horsepower, Mandelbrot put legions of machines to work visualizing fractals. One such man-made fractal, now called the Mandelbrot set, starts with a simple formula, $z^2 + c$. You pick a complex number c, plug in $z = 0$, plug in the result for z again, and continue, at each step plugging the result of the previous step into the formula. The sequence of numbers resulting from this infinitely recursive process turns out to be something of a skeleton key for computing mathematical chaos. One reviewer of Mandelbrot's memoir described this fractal's shape as "a warty snowman or beetle." Zooming in for the self-similar close-up, he elaborated: "a wondrous world of beetle-shaped blobs surrounded by exploding buds, tendrils, curlicues, stylized seahorses, and dragon-like creatures, all bound together by a skein of rarefied filaments."

Fractal geometry now explains events, phenomena, and objects both natural and man-made. To cite some of the odder applications: fractally shaped antennae deliver vastly improved reception. Fractals have infiltrated the recipe for concrete, radically increasing its durability. Most of the <u>rugged Computer-Generated Imagery (CGI) landscapes</u> in Hollywood films are computer-generated with fractals.

One mathematician, Ron Eglash, has even studied how fractal patterns organize the layouts of villages throughout Africa. From an aerial view, you can see how the houses repeat, in self-similar style, a pattern of rings within rings within rings. The central ring is the chief's enclosure, surrounded by his immediate family and extended family beyond that. Inside the chief's compound is an altar with

■ <u>infinite cauliflower</u>: Other edible infinite planes: honeycombs filled with honey. Why are these always hexagonally patterned? See page 90.

✎ <u>rugged Computer-</u>
■ <u>Generated Imagery (CGI) landscapes</u>: Other famous instances of fakery in pattern include "striped paint" (page 69) and

almost the entire history of plaid (page 72).

a model of spirit people, the community's ancestors, also living eternally in fractal organization. As one penetrates the inner sanctum, "you have to get more and more polite," Eglash explained in a 2007 Technology, Entertainment, Design (TED) talk. "So they're mapping the social scaling onto the geometric scaling; it's a conscious pattern."

Mandelbrot's achievements created a sort of patterned lens through which we can see the world anew. "People who just like to look out the window when they fly—they tell me that they see mountains differently now than before," he told *Nova* in 2005. "They see an orderliness to mountains, piles upon piles of pyramids that before they did not see."

Transcendental Numbers

Is the universe ruled more by chaos or by order? Put another way: Does the universe contain more pattern, or more patternlessness? If you believe that the universe is perfectly explained through numbers—a concept captured by Pythagoras' dictum "all is number"—you can frame this question even more precisely: How many numbers are totally patternless?

If a bookie were to come calling and demand a bet, one would be inclined to favor pattern's odds. After all, pattern-making is math's business. Mathematicians aren't just rooting hard for pattern, they're out on the playing field, actively recruiting more numbers and concepts for the "patterned" team. Can we score any quick points for its unruly, patternless twin? Well, the whole category of

irrational numbers is patternless. These include any number that exists as a crisp fraction but, when converted into decimal form, rambles on ceaselessly without any discernible repeat. Score one point for patternlessness.

But it turns out irrational numbers—shaggy and undisciplined as they may seem—fit into a larger paradigm, a jagged piece in a bigger jigsaw pattern. To understand the vastness of this jigsaw, let's imagine a mathematical game whose object is to reduce every number to zero. You're only allowed to use whole numbers and four basic math operations: adding, subtracting, multiplying, and raising the whole kit-and-caboodle to any exponential power you like (provided that exponent is also a whole number). Start with some easy-peasy integer like 7. Getting back to zero is simple: just subtract 7. Now try a fraction, like ⅔: another laughably simple task to reduce to zero. Next choose a funkier number, like the square root of 2. Square that baby, then subtract two and boom: you're back to zero. You've just taken a famous irrational number, the Charlie Sheen of patternlessness, and shunted it squarely into the "patterned" column. Even truly bizarro numbers like the square root of -1 (the definition of an "imaginary" number) or the sum of two weird square roots—both of those reduce nicely to zero.

These numbers have practically nothing in common save one thing: they're all *algebraic*—that is, they're the solution to a polynomial equation with integer coefficients. They're patterned according to the rules of algebra. But here's the surprising part: In the great ocean of all possible numbers, only a few Great Lakes-full are algebraic. All the other numbers fall into another, patternless category: They're

transcendental. Pi belongs to this group, as does the number e, another famous number used to calculate compound interest and measure other kinds of proliferating growth.

How does one navigate a patternless number? Gropingly, and with extraordinary effort. In his memoir *Born on a Blue Day*, autistic savant Daniel Tammet describes how he used his synesthesia to memorize pi to 22,500 decimal places. Picturing the non-repeating pattern in pi as a mental landscape of colors, shapes, and textures, Tammet captured the random order of pi's digits.

Tammet's synesthesia did the job. In just over five hours in 2004, he recited 22,514 nonrepeating digits of pi from memory, setting a new European record. Moral: patternless numbers are daunting, and their patternlessness may not feel like home, but you can make yourself comfy there, until your transcendental patch joins up again with the patterned grid that is Known Math.

Transcendental numbers are fantastically named, but in fact they're the opposite of special. Every transcendental number that touches the known world of mathematics tends to suck that neatly patterned world into its disorganized maw. For instance, we can't even say for sure if adding pi and e together equals a transcendental number (or not). The algebraic numbers populate the workaday world and reassert pattern at every turn: comforting, tame, sensible. But they are far outnumbered by the transcendentals, awaiting only the discovery of a new pattern to illuminate them.

3.14159265358979323846264338327950288419716939937510582

09749445923078164062862089986280348253421170679821480

36513282306647093844609550582231725359408128481117450 2

34102701938521105559644622948954930381964428810975665 9

33446128475648233786783165271201909145648566923460348 6

10454326648213393607260249141273724587006606315588174 8

31520920962829254091715364367892590360011330530548820 4

66521384146951941511609433057270365759591953092186117 3

31932611793105118548074462379962749567351885752724891 2

27938183011949129833673362440656643086021394946395224 7

37190702179860943702770539217176293176752384674818467

66940513200056812714526356082778577134275778960917363 7

78721468440901224953430146549585371050792279689258923

35420199561121290219608640344181598136297747713099605 1

37072113499999998372978049951059731732816096318595024 45

94553469083026425223082533446850352619311881710100031

37838752886587533208381420617177669147303598253490428 7

55468731159562863882353787593751957781857780532171226

30661300192787661119590921642019893809525720106548586 6

32788659361533818279682303019520353018529689957736225

99413891249721775283479131515574857242454150695950829 5

33116861727855889075098381754637464939319255060400927

70167113900984882401285836160356370766010471018194295

55961989467678374494482553797747268471040475346462080

16684259069491293313677028989152104752162056966024058

```
0381501935112533824300355876402474964732639141992726042€
7498385054945885869269956909272107975093029553211653449€
8184175746728909777727938000816470600161452491921732172€
9073941433345477624168625189835694855620992192221842725€
9766814541009538837863609506800642251252051173929848960€
1237137869609563643719172874677646575739624138908658326€
5224894077267194782684826014769909026401363944374553050€
3874105978859597729754989301617539284681382686838689427€
7362226260991246080512438843904512441365497627807977156€
4560285060168427394522674676788952521385225499546667278€
4794510965960940252288797108931456691368672287489405601€
7818931297848216829989487226588048575640142704775551323€
4271661021359695362314429524849371871101457654035902799€
5064302184531910484810053706146806749192781911979399520€
2397489409071864942319615679452080951465502253160388193
5014215030680384477345492026054146659252014974428507325€
6587969981635747363840525714591028970641401109712062804€
1205329281918261861258673215791984148488291644706095752€
9353965725121083579151369882091444210067510334671103141€
9099898599823873455283316355076479185358932261854896321€
9244889575712828905923233260972997120844335732654893823€
2765618093773444030707469211201913020330380197621101100€
7262433441893039686426243410773226978028073189154411010€
0653109896526918620564769312570586356620185581007293606€
5560845529654126654085306143444318586769751456614068007€
```

```
96782354781636009341721641219924586315030286182974555706
55960236480665499119881834797753566369807426542527862551
50141441973568548161361157352552133475741849468438523323
56887671790494601653466804988627232791786085784383827967
88626945604241965285022210661186306744278622039194945047
13390478027590099465764078951269468398352595709825822620
96252451749399651431429809190659250937221696461515709858
91855925245953959431049972524680845987273644695848653836
97700129616089441694868555848406353422072225828488648158
56596116354886230577456498035593634568174324112515076069
08617928680920874760917824938589009714909675985261365549
51523746234364542858444795265867821051141354735739523113
42007310578539062198387447808478489683321445713868751943
53428754440643745123718192179998391015919561814675142691
93762137855956638937787083039069792077346722182562599661
02132434088190710486331734649651453905796268561005508106
69515677157700420337869936007230558763176359421873125147
22091756711672291098169091528017350671274858322287183520
36990865851639831501970165151168517143765761835155650884
89857064204675259070915481416549859461637180270981994309
59746366730583604142813883032038249037589852437441702913
21516084244485963766983889522868478312355265821314495 7685
25271620105265227211166039666557309254711055785376346682
36117910453348850346113657686753249441668039626579787718
77659134401712749470420562230538994561314071127000407854
```

Thanks To . . .

Patternalia got its start in a 2009 *Print* feature, encouraged by my editors James Gaddy and Emily Gordon. I loved the idea of gazing deeply into a wordless pattern and seeing how many stories I could find lurking there: the many patterns globally that resemble this one, the cultural contexts and stories that surround those patterns, all the meanings that stuck to it, explaining the illogical feeling we have that patterns have distinct personalities. But I wasn't at all sure it could be accomplished at book length.

So I pitched a proof-of-concept story about polka dots to *Slate*, which—thanks to editors Hanna Rosin and Jessica Dweck—turned into a fun, surprisingly meaty sample chapter for this book. Still not quite convinced, I plunged into another pattern-story about camouflage that appeared online in the *Believer*. Thanks to editor Hayden Bennett for receiving the idea enthusiastically and firming it up. My blog for *Print* gives me an online forum to pursue all kinds of story ideas, thanks to the editorial support of Jess Farris, Jessica Kuhn, and Zachary Petit. Between these venues, my confidence grew that this book could indeed happen.

I worked with a fantastic publishing team on my first book, *ROY G. BIV: An Exceedingly Surprising Book About Color*—and we got the band back together for *Patternalia*. The Bloomsbury team is top-notch on both sides of the Atlantic. Ros Ellis, Megan Ernst, Natalie Hunt, Laura Keefe, Anthony LaSasso, Tess Viljoen, and especially Rachel Mannheimer, Laura Phillips, and Patti Ratchford: you guys are, singly and collectively, great. And without crucial assistance from my agent Jen Carlson and Yishai Seidman, the magic just don't happen.

This book demanded more research chops than I had going into the project. I thank all the librarians and archivists who received my research "queries" in a spirit of adventure, pointed me in intriguing directions, and helped whip my skills into shape. At Yale's Sterling Memorial Library and the Beinecke Rare Book and Manuscript Library, I thank Robert Carlucci, Remi Castonguay, and Holly Hatheway; at the archives of the Cooper Hewitt, Smithsonian Design Museum, thanks go to Jen Colman and Kimberly Randall. Numerous people deserve thanks at the Textile Museum in Washington, D.C.: Cyndi Bohlin, Katy Clune, Lydia Fraser, and Lee Talbot. Leigh Wishner, formerly of the Cora Ginsburg Gallery in New York, singlehandedly jump-started my research on polka dots; her early assist emboldened me to dig further. Other helpful librarians and archivists I thank include Jenny Lister at the Victoria and Albert Museum in London; Karen DePauw at the Connecticut Historical Society; Melanie Emerson at the Ryerson and Burnham Libraries at the Art Institute of Chicago (and my buddy Emily Robichaud, who introduced us); Lisa Schoblasky at the Newberry Library in Chicago; and various good folks at the Fashion Institute of Technology (FIT) in New York City.

While I hoped my exploration of pattern would sprawl into many disciplines, design- and textile-historians, curators, and practicing designers provided necessary ballast and grounding. In this group I thank Roy Behrens, Rick Beyer, Regina Lee Blaszczyk, Jonathan Faiers, Michelle Fifi, Beverly Gordon, Catherine Harper, Nicole and Petra Kapitza, Grace Lees-Maffei, Sarah Moore, Tim Newark, Elise Ridenour, Pamela Saalbach, Rebecca M. Trussell, and Patricia Williams. Cheers to PATTERNITY in London (Gemma Jones, Anna Murray, and Grace Winteringham) for including me in their 2013 exhibit on stripes. You gave me the perfect excuse to work on that chapter (and revisit London).

Other experts outside the textile and design worlds provided assistance, from idea-bouncing to fact-checking. This group includes Dan Butts, Thomas Carlson, Mark Changizi, Steven Connor, Darra Goldstein, Edward

Hubbard, Douglas MacAyeal, Angela McShane, Sidney Nagel, and Steve Shevell.

I'm lucky to have many nerdy, imaginative friends who helped greatly in theorizing this book. Each of the following buddies can claim a free-drink coupon, redeemable anywhere from Berlin to Chicago (and points beyond): Daniel Albright, Ethan Basch, Tina Boesch, Kimberly Bradley, Bianca Charamsa, Gavin Chuck, Ryan Dohoney and Bryan Markowitz, Claudia Edwards and David Levin, Heidi Enzian, Robert Fink, Jonah and Gabe Gaster, Lisa Kaplan, Chrish Klose, Karin Melnick, Thomas Richter, Josh and Jen Rutner, Haun Saussy and Olga Solovieva, Dave Schutter, Sarah Weiss, Noell Howell Wilson, and Larry Zbikowski.

High-five to Team Childcare, who helped me clear a space to write: Alex Gerard, Tova and Rob Vance, and Maria Doina Visan.

Now to family. Joy Goodwin falls in this category. She's a marvelous writer, a great fellow-mom, and a loving friend. My in-laws, the Krugliaks and Brodskys, are a gaggle of smart, avid readers, witty and loyal to the finish. I hope *Patternalia* appeals particularly to you. Stewarts, my Stewarts! (And Weickels too.) You could make fun from a paper bag. I hope *Patternalia* reflects your curiosity, your collective (ample) sense of humor, and your generous good natures. Here are your names in glittering marquee lights: Mike and Mary Jude Stewart, Andrew and Danielle Stewart, Emily and Maggie Stewart.

Lev! Fraunchy Squishito! Thanks for initiating me as mascot into Club Ginger. You're a joy to parent, and the fun is only just starting. I love watching your little personality unfold, and it tickles me to think you'll read this book (and hopefully many others) one day. I love you very much.

Seth Brodsky, this is your blush-making paragraph. So the most extraordinary person I've ever met agreed to marry me. How lucky is that? Your outsize intelligence is bested

only by your humor and generosity. You may not always feel this way, but to me you're the very model of a great thinker: imaginative and large in your questions; relentless, surprising, and always satisfying in your answers. You are devouringly creative, supportive, enthusiastic. (Adjectives upon adjectives, Desquí!) I even love all our irascible, virtual roommates: Adorno, Lacan, Spahlinger. You make life both tasty and surprising. I love you, friend, and am extremely happy to dedicate this book to you.

Acknowledgments

I extend special thanks to the following people for their kind permission to use copyrighted material as follows:

In the "Dots & Spots" chapter, the quoted text from Yayoi Kusama's performance series *The Anatomic Explosion* is reprinted with the artist's permission.

In the "Lines & Stripes" chapter, the quoted section from *Uyghur Folk-Lore and Legend*, edited by John David Halsted (London: Abela Publishing, 2009), is reprinted with the author's permission.

Also in this chapter, the quoted text from *How the Zebra Got His Stripes: An African Folktale* by Cari Mostert (Create Space Independent Publishing Platform, 2012) is reprinted with the author's permission.

In the "Off the Grid" chapter, quotes from *Symmetry: The Ordering Principle* by David Wade (New York: Walker Publishing, 2006) are reprinted with the publisher's permission © David Wade 2006, Walker Books, an imprint of Bloomsbury Publishing Inc.

Also in this chapter, the quoted section about khipu from *Textiles: The Whole Story: Uses, Meanings, Significance* by Beverly Gordon (New York: Thames & Hudson, 2011) is reprinted with the author's permission. *Textiles: The Whole*

Story by Beverly Gordon copyright © 2011 Beverly Gordon. Reprinted with the kind permission of Thames & Hudson Ltd., London.

Also in this chapter, the quote from *Born on a Blue Day: Inside the Extraordinary Mind of an Autistic Savant* (New York: Free Press, 2007) was reprinted with the author's permission.

Selected Bibliography

The following list of books gathers the titles I found useful enough on the subject of pattern to cite in notes more than once. It also includes relevant titles on the topic that aren't cited directly in this book but would prove valuable to anyone seeking a fuller exploration about pattern.

Introduction, A Crash Course in Pattern, & Off the Grid

Morris & Co. *A brief sketch of the Morris Movement and the firm founded by William Morris to carry out his designs and the industries revived or started by him.* Privately self-published. London: Morris & Company, 1911.

Albarn, Keith, Jenny Miall Smith, Stanford Steele, and Dinah Walker. *The Language of Pattern: An Enquiry Inspired by Islamic Decoration.* London: Thames and Hudson, 1974.

Ball, Philip. *Nature's Patterns: A Tapestry in Three Parts: Flow.* Oxford, England: Oxford University Press, 2009.

Deręgowski, J. B. *Illusions, Patterns and Pictures: A Cross-Cultural Perspective.* London: Academic Press, 1980.

Entwistle, E. A. *A Literary History of Wallpaper.* London: William Clowes and Sons for B. T. Batsford, 1960.

Field, Robert. *Geometric Patterns from Islamic Art & Architecture.* Norfolk, England: Tarquin Publications, 2000.

Hargittai, István, and Magdolna Hargittai. *Symmetry: A Unifying Concept.* Bolinas, California: Shelter Publications, Inc., 1994.

Justema, William. *Pattern: A Historical Panorama.* Boston: New York Graphic Society, 1976.

Lederman, Leon M., and Christopher T. Hill. *Symmetry and the Beautiful Universe.* Amherst, New York: Prometheus Books, 2004.

Meehan, Aidan. *Celtic Design: The Tree of Life.* New York: Thames & Hudson, 1995.

Pastoureau, Michel. *Heraldry: An Introduction to a Noble Tradition.* Translated by Francisca Garvie. New York: Harry N. Abrams, 1997.

———. *Traité d'Héraldique.* Paris: Éditions A. et J. Picard, 1979.

Proctor, Richard M. *The Principles of Pattern for Craftsmen and Designers.* New York: Van Nostrand Reinhold, 1969.

Roberts, Lucienne, and Julia Thrift. *The Designer and the Grid.* Hove, England: RotoVision, 2005.

Slater, Stephen. *The Complete Book of Heraldry: An International History of Heraldry and Its Contemporary Uses.* London: Hermes House, 2003.

Sutton, Daud. *Islamic Pattern: A Genius for Geometry.* New York: Walker & Co., 2007

Van der Post, Lucia. *William Morris and Morris & Co.* London: V&A Publications, 2003.

Wade, David. *Pattern in Islamic Art.* London and New York: Studio Vista, 1976.

———. *Symmetry: The Ordering Principle.* New York: Walker Publishing, 2006.

Washburn, Dorothy K. and Donald W. Crowe. *Symmetries of Culture: Theory and Practice of Plane Pattern Analysis.* Seattle and London: University of Washington Press, 1988.

Lines & Stripes

Hampshire, Mark, and Keith Stephenson. *Communicating with Pattern: Stripes.* Hove, England: RotoVision SA, 2006.

McElroy, Gil. *Razzle Dazzle: The Uses of Abstraction.* Oshawa, Ontario, Canada: The Robert McLaughlin Gallery, 2008.

Pastoureau, Michel, *The Devil's Cloth: A History of Stripes.* Translated by Jody Gladding. New York: Columbia University Press with Washington Square Press, 2003.

Ross, Doran H. *Wrapped in Pride: Ghanaian Kente and African American Identity.* Los Angeles: UCLA Fowler Museum of Cultural History Textile Series, 1998.

Squares & Checks

Faiers, Jonathan. *Tartan.* Oxford, England and New York: Berg Publishers with the Victoria & Albert Museum, 2008.

Hampshire, Mark, and Keith Stephenson. *Communicating with Pattern: Squares, Checks and Grids.* Hove, England: RotoVision, 2007.

Zaczek, Iain. *The History of Tartan.* London: Southwater / Anness Publishing, Ltd. 2005.

Curves & Florals

Behrens, Roy. *Art & Camouflage: Concealment and Deception in Nature, Art and War.* Cedar Falls, Iowa: North American Review, University of Northern Iowa, 1981.

———. *False Colors: Art, Design and Modern Camouflage.* Dysart, Iowa: Bobolink Books, 2008.

Blechman, Hardy. *Disruptive Pattern Material: An Encyclopedia of Camouflage.* London: DPM Ltd, 2004.

Forbes, Peter. *Dazzled and Deceived: Mimicry and Camouflage.* New Haven, Connecticut: Yale University Press, 2009.

Goodden, Henrietta. *Camouflage and Art: Design for Deception in World War 2.* London: Unicorn Press, 2007.

Hope, Dale, with Gregory Tozian. *The Aloha Shirt: Spirit of the Islands.* Hillsboro, Oregon: Beyond Words Publishing, Inc., 2000.

Irwin, John. *The Kashmir Shawl.* London: Victoria & Albert Museum and Her Majesty's Stationery Office (HMSO), 1974.

Lévi-Strauss, Monique. *The Cashmere Shawl.* Photographs by Massimo Listri. Translated by Sara Harris. New York: Harry N. Abrams, 1988.

Newark, Tim. *Camouflage.* New York: Thames & Hudson, 2007.

Newark, Tim, and Quentin Newark, with Dr. D. F. Borsarello. *Brassey's Book of Camouflage.* London: Brassey's, 1996.

Owen, Denis. *Survival in the Wild: Camouflage and Mimicry.* Chicago: University of Chicago Press, 1982.

Rehman, Sherry. *The Kashmiri Shawl: From Jamavar to Paisley.* Woodbridge: Antique Collectors Club, 2005.

Reilly, Valerie, and Frank Ames. *The Paisley Pattern: The Official Illustrated History.* Salt Lake City, Utah: Peregrine Smith Books, 1989.

Stanley, Roy M. II. *To Fool a Glass Eye.* Shrewsbury, England: Airlife Publishing Ltd. 1998.

Steele, H. Thomas. *The Hawaiian Shirt: Its Art and History.* New York: Abbeville Press, 1984.

Yale University Art Gallery. *The Kashmir Shawl.* New Haven, Connecticut: Yale University Art Gallery, 1975.

Textile & Decorative Art Histories

Christie, Archibald H. *Traditional Methods of Pattern Designing: An Introduction to the Study of the Decorative Art.* Oxford, England: Clarendon Press, 1910.

Evans, Joan. *Pattern: A Study of Ornament in Western Europe from 1180 to 1900.* Oxford, England: Clarendon Press, 1931.

Gordon, Beverly. *Textiles: The Whole Story: Uses, Meanings, Significance.* New York: Thames & Hudson, 2011.

Harper, Catherine, ed. *Textile: The Journal of Cloth and Culture* (Bloomsbury).

———. *Textiles: Critical and Primary Sources.* London and New York: Berg Publishers, 2012.

Jones, Owen. *The Grammar of Ornament.* New York: Ivy Press Limited, 2001.

Schoeser, Mary. *World Textiles: A Concise History.* London: Thames & Hudson, 2003.

Interlink Books. *World Textiles: A Sourcebook.* Northampton, Massachusetts: Interlink Books, 2011.

Repeating Motifs & Symbols

Biedermann, Hans. *The Dictionary of Symbolism* trans. James Hulbert. New York and Oxford, England: Facts on File, 1992.

Craycroft, Anna. *Developing Patterns*, Livingston Manor, New York: Evil Twin Publications, 2011.

Heller, Steven. *The Swastika: Symbol Beyond Redemption?* New York: Allworth Press, 2008.

Larwood, Jacob, and Hotten, John Camden. *History of Signboards From the Earliest Times to the Present Day.* London: Chatto & Windus, 1908.

Ronnberg, Ami, editor-in-chief, and Kathleen Martin, editor. *The Book of Symbols: Reflections on Archetypal Images.* Cologne, Germany and London: Taschen, 2010.

Tresidder, Jack, ed. *The Complete Dictionary of Symbols.* London and San Francisco, California: Duncan Baird Publishers and Chronicle Books, 2005

Notes

All books listed in the selected bibliography are cited in short form below. Any other books not listed in the bibliography include a full citation. Each note corresponds to a single entry in the main text unless otherwise noted.

Introduction

10   Proctor, 8–9; Justema, 7–14; Wade (*Symmetry: The Ordering Principle*), 2–9.

11   You can read the original German essay by Loos here: http://de.wikisource.org/wiki/Ornament_und_Verbrechen. This quote is my translation.

A Crash Course in Pattern: The Basics

11   Architecture makes a close second. I've chosen to borrow more from textile histories because pattern is often structurally central to a textile, not a decorative element added later. But devotees of pattern can find scope for further exploration in the bibliography on page 000.

14   Patterns & textiles: like PB&J, Textiles 1-2-3, and The changing anatomy of looms: Schoeser (*World Textiles: A Concise History*), 12–13, 20, 24–26, 38, 44, 66, 81–82, 166, 187; Gordon, 133, 193, 227; Reilly and Ames, 24–25. Quote about textile history as a proxy for all industrial technology comes from Sadie Plant, *Zeroes and Ones: Digital Women and the New Technoculture* (New York: Doubleday, 1997), 15, 61, 64. This video shows you how to make felt with the wet-mat method: https://www.youtube.com/watch?v=jNMs2LSXq70. Thanks go to Catherine Harper, Dean, Faculty of Creative and Cultural Industries at University of Portsmouth (Portsmouth, England) and editor of *Textile: The Journal of Cloth and Culture*, for correcting my facts in this section.

15   http://www.slate.com/articles/arts/design/2012/03/african_fabric_where_do_tribal_prints_really_come_from_.single.html.

16   Facts on "conversational prints" and *toile de jouy* come from Sonja Andrew, "Textile Semantics: Considering a Communication-Based Reading of Textiles," *Textile* 6, no. 1 (2008): 32–65; see also Gordon, 219–223. View Timorous Beasties' toile collection here: http://www.timorousbeasties.com/collection/toile. On paper dresses: see Kathleen Paton, "Paper dresses" in *A-Z of Fashion* (Berg Fashion Library, online subscription) and http://designgallery.wisc.edu/exhibits/paperdresses/crazyman.html.

19   Gestalt Psychology and Pattern Recognition: Now in Live 3-D Motion!: See http://www.britannica.com/EBchecked/topic/232098/Gestalt-psychology and http://www.scholarpedia.org/article/Gestalt_principles. This Gizmodo article explains closure well: http://www.gizmodo.co.uk/2013/05/why-your-brain-thinks-these-dots-are-a-dog/. Another good summary applying Gestalt principles to interaction design: http://sixrevisions.com/web_design/gestalt-principles-applied-in-design/. Thanks to Dr. Thomas Carlson, Department of Cognitive Science, Macquarie University in Sydney, Australia, for his help in fact-checking this section.

19   See http://www.bbc.com/news/magazine-22686500, http://www.theatlantic.com/technology/archive/2012/08/pareidolia-a-bizarre-bug-of-the-human-mind-emerges-in-computers/260760/, http://www.theguardian.com/science/2013/nov/17/why-we-see-hitler-house, and http://www.psychologytoday.com/blog/reality-play/201207/being-amused-apophenia.

Dots & Spots

24   Most of polka dots' essential backstory I first discovered in a pamphlet, "Why Do You Call Them Polka Dots?," published in 1918 by Connecticut-based textile manufacturers Cheney Silks. You'll find the recipe for polka pudding here: http://chestofbooks.com/food/recipes/Owen-New-Cook-Book/Polka-Pudding.html and for polka sauce here: http://chestofbooks.com/food/recipes/Owen-New-Cook-Book/Polka-Sauce.html. Much of this entry—as well as the entries entitled "Polka Dots, Moonbeams, and Patriotism," "Who Owns Polka Dots?" and "Polka-Dot Bikinis"—first appeared in a slide show I wrote for *Slate*, "Seeing Spots," September 10, 2010: http://www.slate.com/slideshows/double_x/seeing-spots.html. I promise you a rollicking ball touring the polka sheet music from the 1840s to the 1860s, thanks to the Duke University Rare Book, Manuscript, and Special Collections Library: http://library.duke.edu/digitalcollections/ and the Nineteenth-Century American Sheet Music Collection, Music Library, University of North Carolina-Chapel Hill: http://www.lib.unc.edu/dc/sheetmusic/?CISOROOT=/sheetmusic. Later examples, like the "She's Too Fat for Me Polka," are available via the Templeton Digital Sheet Music Collection, Mississippi State University Libraries: http://digital.library.msstate.edu/collections/sheetmusic/index.html.

25   "Polka Dot Called Uncopyrightable," Special to the *New York Times*, April 11, 1936. For more info on the Duffy bill and Vanderberg amendment to same, see "The Thirty-Ninth Annual Report of the Register of Copyrights for the Fiscal Year Ending June 30, 1936" by the Library of Congress Copyright Office, http://www.copyright.gov/reports/annual/archive/ar-1936.pdf. Copyrighting patterns has historically proven a hard sell in juridical circles. In 2010, fashion retailer Express sued Forever 21 for ripping off four of its supposedly copyrighted plaids.

Express lost the suit when it became clear they had themselves copied these plaids from a (supposedly lost) preexisting design, with zero alterations between any of the versions. Evan Clark, "Judge Rules for Forever 21 in Express Copyright Case," *Women's Wear Daily (WWD)* September 7, 2010.

28 Sylva Weaver, "Polka Dots Fly in Spring Style Breeze," *Los Angeles Times*, March 11, 1940. Jeanne Contini, "Fashion Find: Coin of the Realm or Your Money's Worth," *Washington Post*, April 7, 1943.

28 "'Girl in Polka Dots' Surrenders in L.A.," *Daytona Beach Morning Journal* via Associated Press, June 8, 1989: http://news. google.com/newspapers?id=KWUpAAAAI BAJ&sjid=f8kEAAAAIBAJ&pg=.&dq=pol ka-dots&hl=en.

29 Very first bikinis: Prithvi Kumar Agrawala, *Goddesses in Ancient India* (New Delhi: Abhinav Publications, 1984), 12. Ovid on bikinis: Liza Cleland, Glenys Davies, and Lloyd Llewellyn-Jones, *Greek and Roman Dress from A to Z* (Oxon, England and New York: Routledge, 2007). Twentieth-century introduction of bikinis: http://www.history. com/this-day-in-history/bikini-introduced and http://www.metmuseum.org/toah/hd/ biki/hd_biki.htm. Brian Hyland's song: Fred Bronson, *The Billboard Book of #1 Hits*, 5th ed. (New York: Billboard Publications, 2003), 72.

30 See Steven Connor, "Maculate Conceptions," *Textile: The Journal of Cloth and Culture* 1 (2003): 49–63.

31 Medieval bestiaries on panthers: *Etymologies*, Book 12, 2:8–9, as referenced here: http:// bestiary.ca/beasts/beast79.htm. See also John David Halsted, ed., *Uyghur Folk-Lore and Legend*, (London: Abela Publishing, 2009), 29–32.

32 From http://dc.wikia.com/wiki/Abner_Krill_ (New_Earth).

34 http://www.culturalsurvival.org/publications/ cultural-survival-quarterly/botswana/ hallucinogenic-plants-and-their-use-traditional-so. See also Marlene Dobkin De Rios, "Enigma of Drug-Induced Altered States of Consciousness Among the !Kung Bushmen of the Kalahari Desert," *Journal of Ethnopharmacology* 15, no. 3, (March 1986): 297–304. Abstract accessible here: http:// www.ncbi.nlm.nih.gov/pubmed/3724210. See also Thomas A. Dowson, "Dots and Dashes: Cracking the Entoptic Code in Bushmen Rock Paintings." South African Archaeological Society. Goodwin's Legacy (June 1989): 84–94.

34 This description of the *lutumbo lwa kindi* initiations in Kabila village of Congo (Democratic Republic) derives from captions to photographs by Eliot Elisofon, on assignment for *Life* magazine from August to December 1959, Smithsonian Institution, National Museum of African Art, Eliot Elisofon Photographic Archives, local # EEPA EECL 5284, F 3 LGA 1 EE 59. Much of this entry—as well as the entries entitled "Polka Dots, Moonbeams and Patriotism," "Who Owns Polka Dots?," "Polka-Dotted Bikinis," and "Patching and Mole-Reading"—first appeared in a slideshow I wrote for *Slate*, "Seeing Spots," September 10, 2010: http://www.slate.com/slideshows/ double_x/seeing-spots.html.

35 See Audrey Yoshiko Seo, *Ensō: Zen Circles of Enlightenment*. Foreword by John Daido Loori. (Boston: Weatherill, 2007) or this website: http://www.shakuhachizen.com/ ensoenglish.html. The story of Giotto's perfect circle appears in the *Ensō* book foreword with further elaborations from author William Landay here: http://www. williamlanday.com/2010/10/05/drawing-circles/#.UMC9uZPjnXU

38 About the Galton box: See Michael Bulmer, *Francis Galton: Pioneer of Heredity and Biometry* (Baltimore: Johns Hopkins University Press, 2003). Five T's from Douglas D. Dave, *A Law Enforcement Sourcebook of Asian Crime and Cultures: Tactics and Mindsets* (Boca Raton, FL: CRC Press, 1997),113: http:// books.google.com/books?id=Z0k0kTGivP4 C&source=gbs_navlinks_s. Other meanings from Steve Gilbert, *Tattoo History: A Source Book: An Anthology of Historical Records of Tattooing Throughout the World* (Juno Books, 2000), 153. About the electric tattoo pen: http://blog.nyhistory.org/edison-and-the-tattoo/.

41 The Brooklyn Children's Museum exhibit on African textiles is a great place to start learning about both adinkra symbols and kente patterns: http://www.brooklynkids. org/attachments/BCMWB_PCP_ AfricanTextiles.pdf. The adinkra motifs mentioned in this entry are all defined here: http://www.adinkra.org/htmls/adinkra_ index.htm.

42 All the delicious tidbits on patching come from an essay on spots by Steven Connor, "Maculate Conceptions" in *Textile: The Journal of Cloth and Culture* 1 (2003): 49–63. More info on "longing marks" and the European method of fortune-telling with moles can be found in Connor's book *The Book of Skin* (London: Reaktion; and Ithaca, NY: Cornell University Press, 2004), especially pages 96–98 and 304.

42 http://pressblog.uchicago.edu/2012/04/03/ obliterate-wall-street-men-with-polka-dots.html. See also Jo Applin, *Yayoi Kusama: Infinity Mirror Room—Phalli's Field*, (London: Afterall Books, 2012); http:// www.brooklynrail.org/2012/04/art_books/ kusama-in-her-own-words; and http://www. artdaily.org/section/news/index.asp?int_ sec=2&int_new=19144#.UXBJAC.

Lines & Stripes

48 This entry is indebted to Michel Pastoureau, *The Devil's Cloth: A History of Stripes*. He relates the story of the Carmelites on pages 7–11, discusses Leviticus on pages 2–3, and explains medieval Europeans' way of "reading" visuals on pages 19–26.

48 Etymology of words meaning "stripe": Pastoureau (*The Devil's Cloth*), 59–60. Hampshire and Stephenson, 68. On prisoners' stripes and alternative looks, see http://www.slate.com/articles/news_and_politics/explainer/2010/12/orange_alert.html.

49 From Michel Pastoureau, (*Heraldry*), 14–15, 17, 19; and Slater, 14–17, 22–27, 36–37. For modern uses of heraldry, see Slater, 178, 223, 239; and Pastoureau (*Heraldry*), 92–95.

51 Slater, 52–53, 72–73, 82–83, 89, 98–99, 107, 122–123; Pastoureau (*Heraldry*), 43, 46–48, 84–88, 131.

51 Pastoureau (*Heraldry*), 41, 69–71; Hampshire and Stephenson, 48.

52 Pastoureau (*Heraldry*), 48–53.

52 Hampshire and Stephenson, 70, and http://dictionary.com. The latter source defines twill as "one of the basic weave structures in which the filling threads are woven over and under two or more warp yarns, producing a characteristic diagonal pattern."

53 Ibid., 44–47.

54 See http://www.nytimes.com/2006/04/20/fashion/thursdaystyles/20CODES.html?_r=2&. For the etymology of seersucker, see *The American Heritage Dictionary of the English Language*, 5th ed. (Boston: Houghton Mifflin Harcourt Publishing Company, 2014), available

online: https://ahdictionary.com/word/search.html?q=seersucker. On Seersucker Thursday, http://www.washingtonpost.com/opinions/dana-milbank-the-seersucker-bond-unraveled/2012/06/26/gJQArzoJ5V_story.html?tid=wp_ipad.

54 Facts for this entry also came from an e-mail exchange with Lee Talbot, curator of the Eastern Hemisphere collection of the Textile Museum in Washington, D.C., supplemented by this webpage of the Manitoba Crafts Museum and Library (accessed November 26, 2014): http://www.mcml.ca/a-true-princes-coat/.

55 From Patrick Newman, *Tracking the Weretiger: Supernatural Man-Eaters of India, China and Southeast Asia* (Jefferson, NC: McFarland & Co., 2012).

56 See http://discovermagazine.com/2013/jan-feb/67-tiger-stripes-explained; Ami Ronnberg and Kathleen Martin, eds., *The Book of Symbols* (Taschen, 2010), 270; Hans Biedermann, *The Dictionary of Symbolism*, trans. James Hulbert (Facts on File, 1992), 344–345; and Jack Tresidder, ed., *The Complete Dictionary of Symbols*, (Duncan Baird Publishers and Chronicle Books, 2005), 478.

57 The 2012 study is summarized in http://www.economist.com/node/21547216; the original study, by A. Egri, M. Blahó, G. Kriska, R. Farkas, M. Gyurkovszky, S. Akesson, G. Horváth, bears the less-than-friendly title, "Polarotactic Tabanids Find Striped Patterns with Brightness and/or Polarization Modulation Least Attractive: An Advantage of Zebra Stripes," *The Journal of Experimental Biology* 215 (March 1, 2012):736–45. doi: 10.1242/jeb.065540. A related 2010 study by basically the same team explains why all-white animals repel flies most effectively: "An Unexpected Advantage of Whiteness in Horses:

The Most Horsefly-proof Horse Has a Depolarizing White Coat," G. Horváth, M. Blahó, G. Kriska, R. Hegedüs, B. Gerics, R. Farkas, S. Akesson, *Proceedings of the Royal Society B—Biological Sciences* 277: 1688 (June 7, 2010):1643–1650. doi: 10.1098/rspb.2009.2202. If that's not enough nerd-food for you, try this 2014 study that took these findings a step further, proving a strong statistical correlation between equids with distinct stripes and areas where parasites are most active. See: http://www.independent.co.uk/news/science/why-do-zebras-have-stripes-biologists-say-they-finally-have-the-answer-9232098.html; original article here: http://www.nature.com/ncomms/2014/140401/ncomms4535/full/ncomms4535.html. For the full African folktale, see Cari Mostert, *How the Zebra Got His Stripes: African Folk Tales* (CreateSpace Independent Publishing Platform, 2012).

60 I first learned of the Beast in Pastoureau, *The Devil's Cloth*, 24–25, and enlarged my understanding with Jay M. Smith, *Monsters of the Gévaudan: The Making of a Beast* (Cambridge, MA: Harvard University Press, 2011). Devotees of the Beast will also dig this video recapping the tale in bewigged CSI-reenactment style: https://www.youtube.com/watch?v=1fyTL50hQKM.

61 Much of this entry originally appeared in my blog for *Print* magazine. Sources include Larwood and Hotten, 341–45, and Ebenezer Cobham, *Brewer's Dictionary of Phrase and* Fable, ed. Camilla Rockwood (Edinburgh: Brewer's, 2009).

62 Read Woodland's *New York Times* obituary here: http://www.nytimes.com/2012/12/13/business/n-joseph-woodland-inventor-of-the-bar-code-dies-at-91.html?hp&_r=1& and learn to parse bar codes with this video: https://www.youtube.com/watch?v=e6aR1k-ympo. Although Woodland patented the

circular barcode concept with Bernard Silver in 1952, it took decades for familiar, rectangular barcodes to become standard. In the early 1970s, George J. Laurer designed a rectangular barcode concept with Woodland's input; that design was popularized by supermarket executive Alan Haberman and became the industry standard in 1973. These three articles document the growing funerary-QR code movement: https://web.archive.org/web/20120502174456/, http://www.japantrends.com/qr-code-graves-give-a-memorial-window/, and http://www.bizjournals.com/seattle/blog/2011/04/seattle-company-quiring-monuments-adds.html.

63 *The Stanford Encyclopedia of Philosophy* defines iki: http://plato.stanford.edu/entries/japanese-aesthetics/#6. Thanks to Professor Noell Howell Wilson for telling me about iki's connection to stripes.

64 From John Lloyd and John Mitchinson, *If Ignorance Is Bliss, Why Aren't There More Happy People?: Smart Quotes for Dumb Times* (New York: Harmony Books, 2009).

65 See Gordon, 156. Find specific kente patterns and their meanings at http://exploringafrica.matrix.msu.edu/teachers/curriculum/m12/activity3.php and http://africa.si.edu/exhibits/kente/when.htm and the stories of Nkrumah's kente-wearing at http://www.philamuseum.org/micro_sites/exhibitions/africanart/resource_book/object_text.pdf. I thank independent textile scholar Elise Ridenour for correcting this entry for factual errors. I got the T-shirt slogans mentioned from my mom's personal collection, sourced from none other than the Stewart family business, Fluf n' Stuf. Yes, my father was retail Santa Claus.

68 This entry originally appeared in a series I wrote for the *Believer*: http://logger.believermag.com/post/61681696398/hiding-in-plain-sight-a-visual-history-of-camouflage. See McElroy, 12–13; Tim Newark (*Camouflage*), 74, 78, 88–89; and Blechman, 164, 166, 170.

68 See Gordon, 104. Read more about Zig-Zag rolling papers: http://www.zigzag.com/history.html. Learn about reduplications from the public radio program *A Way with Words* (skip to 3:05): http://www.waywordradio.org/zig-zag-and-shilly-shally/. EUdict gives the Hungarian translation of *zeg-zug*: http://www.eudict.com/?lang=huneng&word=zeg-zug. See the *nkyinkyim* adinkra symbol for yourself here: http://www.adinkra.org/htmls/adinkra/nkyi.htm.

69 Snopes.com did the heavy lifting for this entry: http://www.snopes.com/holidays/christmas/candycane.asp#d3YLpzE3I5VdKLwB.99. R. O. Parker, *Introduction to Food Science* (Albany, NY: Delmar/Internaional Thomson, 2001) is one among many books retelling candy cane legend as fact. Check out the candy cane forming machine patent here: http://www.google.com/patents/US2956520. Sal Ferrara spilled the candy-coated beans of his company's dominance in this interview with *Candy Industry* magazine: http://www.candyindustry.com/articles/85351-one-on-one-with-sal-ferrara. Learn how Blackpool Rock is made here: http://h2g2.com/approved_entry/A4552841.

Squares & Checks

73 Two books proved super-useful in completing my knowledge of tartan-slash-plaid: Jonathan Faiers, *Tartan,* and Iain Zaczek, *The History of Tartan*. For tartan vocabulary, see Faiers 34–37 and Zaczek, 12–15, 91, 101. Faiers recounts the invention of the "little kilt" on page 79.

74 Zaczek, 36–47, as well as Faiers, 107–109

and 53. For more on tartan-madness in portraiture, see Robin Nicholson, "Use of Tartan as a Symbol of Identity," *Textile History* 36, no. 2 (November 2005): 146–167.

74 Faiers, 65–66 and Zaczek 56–58.

74 Faiers, 37–44, 151–154 and Zaczek, 58–61.

76 Faiers, 66–72 and Zaczek 70–71.

76 Faiers, 238, 138, 139–140. *The Atlantic* recaps the history of the modern business suit: http://www.theatlantic.com/national/archive/2012/07/where-did-business-suits-come-from/260182/.

78 Faiers, 156–57, 98.

78 Hampshire and Stephenson, 14.

79 Hampshire and Stephenson, 22–27. The French-German television network ARTE's delightful TV program *Karambolage* did a feature on vichy and *tote Barbès*—here's the transcript of that in French: http://www.arte.tv/fr/l-objet-le-cabas-barbes/3108344,CmC=3108350.html.

79 See http://www.independent.co.uk/life-style/fashion/features/ready-to-wear-houndstooth-is-fierce-and-signifies-power-over-and-above-prettiness-1813062.html, http://www.forbes.com/global/1998/0727/0108008a.html, and http://www.tess-elation.co.uk/houndstooth.

81 See http://www.dailyrecord.co.uk/news/uk-world-news/feared-glasgow-cop-beat-gangs-1004061 and https://www.mi5.gov.uk/home/about-us/who-we-are/staff-and-management/sir-percy-sillitoe.html. See also Hampshire and Stephenson, 54–55; A. McArthur and H. Kingsley Long, *No Mean City* (London: Neville Spearman, 1984); and Sir Percy Sillitoe, *Cloak Without Dagger* (London: Cassell, 1955).

81 The Indian proverb comes from Norman Knight and Will Guy, eds., *King, Queen and Knight: A Chess Anthology in Prose and Verse* (New York: St. Martin's, 1975), 226. I found that citation, along with chess's provenance and global spread, in William N. Rogers II, "Heroic Defense: The Lost Positions of Nabokov's Luzhin and Kawabata's Shūsai," *Comparative Literature Studies* 20, No. 2 (Summer 1983): 217–230. The Oxford English Dictionary puts the earliest mention of "checkers" to the fourteenth century. Dozens of renditions exist of the wheat or rice problem; I've relied on these two: Eli Maor, *To Infinity and Beyond: A Cultural History of the Infinite* (Princeton, NJ: Princeton University Press, 1991), 29–30, and Carl Sagan, *Billions and Billions: Thoughts on Life and Death at the Brink of the Millennium* (New York: Ballantine Books, 1997), chapter 2, "The Persian Chessboard."

81 Gordon, 268.

84 Gordon, 155, as well as Larry Allen, *The Encyclopedia of Money*, (Santa Barbara, CA: ABC-CLIO, 2009), 73.

84 See Fred, Egloff, *Origin of the Checker Flag: A Search for Racing's Holy Grail* (Watkin's Glen: International Motor Racing Research Center, 2006). See also http://www.nascar.com/en_us/sprint-cup-series/nascar-nation/nascar-edu/did-you-know/explaining-the-checkered-flag.html. The *Indy Star/News* story was written by Donald Davidson, "Checkered Flag at the Finish Line Predated Automobiles," May 29, 1999: http://web.archive.org/web/20000306041946/http://speednet.starnews.com/speednet/irl/99/may/0529sn_ddflag.html.

87 See Tineke Rooijakkers, "Palestinian Scarves and Flag Dresses," *Berg Encyclopedia of World Dress and Fashion* 5, part 3. This 2001 interview in the *Guardian* recaps Leila Khaled's role in popularizing the kaffiyeh: http://www.theguardian.com/world/2001/jan/26/israel. See also "Where Some See Fashion, Others See Politics" and http://www.huffingtonpost.com/2008/05/28/dunkin-donuts-pulls-ad-fe_n_103859.html.

87 http://sanaahamid.com/Cultural-Appropriation-A-Conversation

89 See http://www.adinkra.org/htmls/adinkra_index.htm and http://www.adinkra.org/htmls/adinkra/owuo-atwedee.htm. See also Schoeser, *World Textiles: A Concise History* by Mary Schoeser (Thames & Hudson Ltd, 2003), page 148.

89 See http://www.ehow.com/about_5398882_history-loose-leaf-paper.html.

90 Here is Robert Krulwich's NPR piece, http://www.npr.org/blogs/krulwich/2013/05/13/183704091/what-is-it-about-bees-and-hexagons, itself based on a section of the book by Alan Lightman, *The Accidental Universe: The World You Thought You Knew* (New York: Vintage, 2014). Read a layman-friendly explanation of Hales's proof: http://www.maa.org/frank-morgans-math-chat-hales-proves-hexagonal-honeycomb-conjecture.

91 The six faces of a brick are named in Rob W. Sovinski, *Brick in the Landscape: A Practical Guide to Specification and Design* (Hoboken, NJ: John Wiley & Sons, 1999), 43. Also useful: W. G. Nash, *Brickwork* (London: Hutchinson, 1983).

Curves & Florals

95 See this webpage from the Victoria & Albert Museum in London (accessed November 26, 2014), http://www.vam.ac.uk/content/articles/w/william-morris-and-wallpaper-design/, and Fiona MacCarthy, *William Morris: A Life for Our Time* (London: Faber, 1994), 1–2, 7, 17–18, 26–27, 37–40, 52, 56–58, 111–112, 185, 371–372, 412–413, 454–458, 590, 604–605, 631–633. On Morris's influence on fantasy fiction, see the "William Morris" entry in Harold Bloom, ed., *Classic Fantasy Writers* (New York: Chelsea House Publishers, 1994).

95 From Reilly, 10–11. See also Yale University Art Gallery, *The Kashmir Shawl*, 37–38.

105 See Rebecca Wells Corrie, "The Paisley" in Yale University Art Gallery, *The Kashmir Shawl*, 24–48; Michelle Maskiell, "Consuming Kashmir: Shawls and Empires, 1500–2000," *Journal of World History* 13, no. 1 (Spring 2002): 27–28, 32–33; Caroline Karpinski, "Kashmir to Paisley," *The Metropolitan Museum of Art Bulletin*, New Series 22, no. 3 (November 1963): 119; Lévi-Strauss, 15. About the wool: See Gordon, 151 and 177; Reilly, 15–20, 32; Sarah Buie Pauly, "The Shawl: Its Context and Construction" in Yale University Art Gallery, *The Kashmir Shawl*, 9–11; Lévi-Strauss, 14–15.

99 Reilly, 7–9, 12, 20, 32–35, 39–40; Gordon, 177–179; Buie Pauly, 9–10, 14; Karpinski, 116–117, 120–121, 123; Lévi-Strauss, 16, 28–29, 38–39, 48, 52. See also http://www.nytimes.com/1989/06/04/travel/shoppers-world-from-scotland-by-way-of-india-richly-colorful-paisley-shawls.html, http://threadsofhistory.blogspot.com/2009/09/paisley-visual-history.html, and http://www.telegraph.co.uk/travel/destinations/europe/uk/738952/Paisley-a-designer-heritage.html.

102 Reilly, 42; Lévi-Strauss, 52; Gordon, 219. See also http://www.liberty.co.uk/AboutLiberty/article/fcp-content, http://www.vogue.com/vogue-daily/article/paisley-pops-up-again/#1, and http://www.slate.com/blogs/the_eye/2013/10/14/blue_jeans_what_s_the_reason_behind_the_color.html.

On hanky code, see Susan Stryker and Jim Van Buskirk, *Gay By the Bay: A History of Queer Culture in the San Francisco Bay Area* (San Francisco: Chronicle Books, 1996) 18; Larry Townsend, *The Leatherman's Handbook II* (New York: Modernismo Publications, 1983), 26.

71 See Pastoureau (*Traité d'Héraldique*), 160–165; I have translated the Pastoreau quotes into English. Pastoureau later expands and updates this information in *Heraldry: An Introduction to a Noble Tradition* (Thames and Hudson, 1997), 90–91. For an in-depth look into the lily-iris-bee-et-cetera debate, see Maurice Rowland, "Reflecting on the Fleur de Lis in European Heraldic Art," *The Coat of Arms* 13, no 191 (Heraldic Society, 2000): 292–298. Basic facts were also corroborated with the Oxford English Dictionary and *Encyclopædia Britannica* [serial online], accessed April 2014; Available from: Research Starters, Ipswich, MA. Accessed June 24, 2014. For Clovis's history, see http://www.encyclopedia.com/topic/Clovis_I.aspx. The idea of fleur-de-lis symbolizing French social classes comes from George Duby, *France in the Middle Ages 987–1460: From Hugh Capet to Joan of Arc* (Oxford: Blackwell, 1993). See also Slater, 197.

105 E. Cobham Brewer, *Dictionary of Phrase and Fable* (Henry Altemus, 1898; Bartleby.com, 2000) gives Guillim as the source of the three-toad theory: http://www.bartleby.com/81/4298.html. Maurice Rowland discusses toads and frogs on Pharamond's arms on page 293 of his article "Reflecting on the Fleur de Lis in European Heraldic Art," *The Coat of Arms* (Heraldic Society) 13, no. 191 (2000). The more learned sources backing up the Nostradamus story include *Brewer's Dictionary of Phrase and Fable* as well as Rowland. See Wheeler Syndicate, "Why Is 'Jean Crapaud' Symbolic of France?," *Pittsburgh Press*, March 14, 1921:

http://news.google.com/newspapers?id=hx8bAAAAIBAJ&sjid=8kkEAAAAIBAJ&pg=4300%2C5519346. Quote explaining Nostradamus' prophecy comes from William Seward's *Anecdotes of Ditinguished Persons* as cited in *Certain Comeoverers* by Henry Howland Crapo (New Bedford, MA, E. Anthony & Sons, Inc., 1912), full text of which is accessible online here: https://archive.org/stream/certaincomeovere01crap/certaincomeovere01crap_djvu.txt

107 *Fleurdeliser* is documented as early as 1650 by the OED. See also Francis X. Blouin and William G. Rosenberg, *Archives, Documentation, and Institutions of Social Memory: Essays from the Sawyer Seminar* (University of Michigan Press, 2007), 291–292. See also Emilie Bahr, "New Orleans Sees Explosion in Fleur de Lis Tattoos" *Journal of Jefferson Parish*, May 16, 2008. LexisNexis Academic (accessed August 21, 2014).

107 Gordon, 214–215. The spider anecdote comes from an article Gordon cites: Susan Domowitz, "Wearable Proverbs: Anyi Names for Printed Factory Cloth," *African Arts* 25, no. 3 (1992): 84.

108 Gordon, 216, as well as http://prezi.com/6oybkxm3qslw/madagascar-lamba-cloth/ and Rebecca L. Green, "Lamba Hoany: Proverb Cloths from Madagascar," in *African Arts* (Summer 2003): 30–43.

108 Gordon, 216, who cites Patricia L. Hickman, "Turkish Oya," M.A. thesis, University of California-Berkeley, 1977, 44, 47, 54. For more on Ophelia's flowers, see http://www.nytimes.com/1999/02/14/nyregion/gardening-how-to-speak-the-language-of-flowers.html and http://www.sfgate.com/homeandgarden/article/Study-flowers-in-Ophelia-s-garland-to-learn-folk-2542041.php.

109 This section on camouflage first appeared in a five-part series I wrote for the *Believer* Logger, September 17–23, 2013: http://logger.believermag.com/post/61503586468/hiding-in-plain-sight-a-visual-history-of-camouflage. Special thanks go to Roy Behrens, camouflage expert and professor of art at the University of Northern Iowa, for his help with this section.

109 From Behrens (*False Colors*).

111 Miller, Introduction, 12–14, 22–23, 31 in Tim Newark (*Camouflage*) as well as page 72 by Newark (henceforth "Newark and Miller"). See also Blechman, 26–29, 54–55, 74–75 (henceforth "*DPM*"). See also Goodden, 12 (hereinafter "Goodden"). See also Newark, Newark, and Borsarello, 16 (henceforth "*Brassey's*").

111 Khaki's origins: Newark and Miller, 43–46; *Brassey's*, 11–14; *DPM*, 120–123. Nanny of the Maroons: *DPM*, 93.

112 Newark and Miller, 54, 56, 60–62; *DPM*, 25; Goodden, 10.

112 Newark and Miller, 62–65; DPM, 132–135, 159–163. Watch a clip from the Chaplin movie here: https://www.youtube.com/watch?v=6wduJEIZkKs&feature=youtu.be&t=53s.

113 Newark and Miller, 82–87; *DPM*, 154–157, 184.

113 Goodden, 50, who traces the quote's source to a paper by Tom Purvis, *Art and Industry* (November 1959): 200, quoted by John Trevelyn in *Impact of War on Art: War Jobs*. See also *DPM*, 176–177, 180–183.

114 *DPM*, 178–179.

114 *Brassey's*, 28–33, 35; *DPM*, 252. See also http://www.time.com/time/nation/article/0,8599,1906083,00.html and

http://www.theatlantic.com/technology/archive/2011/06/a-brief-history-of-military-camouflage/240291/#slide6.

115 See http://www.wired.com/dangerroom/2007/11/made-to-order-c/, http://content.time.com/time/nation/article/0,8599,1906083,00.html, http://www.theatlantic.com/magazine/archive/2011/07/invisible-inc/308523/2/ and DPM, 254–259.

115 See http://camoupedia.blogspot.com/2011/04/alon-bement-georgia-okeeffes-teacher.html and http://www.smh.com.au/entertainment/art-and-design/how-dupains-nude-helped-the-troops-cover-up-20111216-1oyrd.html

115 DPM, 292–297, 302–303, 306–307, 314–315. See the images mentioned in this section here: http://ideas.ted.com/2013/05/15/11-stunning-images-from-liu-bolin-the-disappearing-man/ and even more on his gallery site: http://www.kleinsungallery.com/artist/liu_bolin/works/.

116 DPM, 96; and http://www.time.com/time/nation/article/0,8599,1906083,00.html.

117 From Ella Wheeler Wilcox, Hello, Boys! (London: Gay and Hancock, 1919), http://www.ellawheelerwilcox.org/poems/pcamoufl.htm.

Off the Grid

121 From Dick Higgins, Pattern Poetry: Guide to an Unknown Literature (State University of New York Press, 1987), 92, 101, 108, 112–122, 153, 157, 179–182, 184–186, 216 and the book's two appendices. On hui-wen, see Kang-i Sun Chang and Haun Saussy eds., Women Writers of Traditional China: An Anthology of Poetry and Criticism (Stanford University Press, 1999), 669–671. I thank Haun Saussy, University Professor in the department of comparative literature at the University of Chicago, for vastly upping both the learned- and hilarity-quotients of this entry. Interestingly, this account of Su Hui's poem was written by Wu Zetian (624/627–705 b.c.e.), China's first and only female ruler. (Go, girl power!) Finally, go a little nutso with palindromes on this online list; I've quoted #46: http://www.derf.net/palindromes/old.palindrome.html.

122 Sutton, 1–9, 12–13, 16–19, 34–35, 40–41, 54–55, 57. See also http://patternislamicart.com/background-notes/the-evolution-of-style, http://www.bbc.co.uk/religion/religions/islam/art/art_1.shtml, and http://artofislamicpattern.com/resources/educational-posters/. The lines quoted from the Koran are from AYAT al-Ahzab 33:21, as rendered by Yusuf Ali (Saudi Rev. 1985) and found online here: http://islamawakened.com/quran/33/21/. On kufic script and Arabic calligraphy generally, see Mangho Ahuja and A. L. Loeb, "Tessellations in Islamic Calligraphy," Leonardo (MIT Press) 28, no. 1 (1995): 41–45. Islamic patterns are so intertwined with geometry, they're now commonly used to teach schoolchildren math principles. See Fayeq S. Oweis, "Islamic Art As an Educational Tool About the Teaching of Islam," Art Education, (National Art Education Association) 55, no. 2 (March 2002): 18–24. On the meanings of the name Ali: http://www.islamic-dictionary.com/index.php?word=ali.

123 From Gordon, 202–205. For more on Ryukyu worker knots, khipu, and German miller knots, see Karl Menninger, Number Terms and Number Symbols: A Cultural History of Numbers (Dover Publications, 1992), 252–256. To see an Asante mpatapo, go here: http://www.symbols.com/symbol/577.

125 All of David Wade, Symmetry: The Ordering Principle, was useful in writing this entry, but particularly pages 8–11, 14–29, 36, 42–43. See also Hargittai and Hargittai, 2–16, 32–33, 200–209, chapter 15. An interesting offshoot of plane divisions is Penrose tiling, a form of non-periodic tiling that fills an infinite plane without using any translation symmetry. Penrose tilings are also self-similar, like fractals, and quasi-crystal. See Wade (Symmetry), 36–37. Thanks to Jonah Gaster, postdoctoral fellow in mathematics at Boston College, and his brother Gabriel Gaster, data scientist at Datascope Analytics, for firming up my facts in this section.

127 See Mandelbrot's New York Times obituary: http://www.nytimes.com/2010/10/17/us/17mandelbrot.html; the New York Review of Books review of his memoir: http://www.nybooks.com/articles/archives/2013/may/23/mandelbrot-mathematics-of-roughness/?pagination=false; Mandelbrot's 2005 Nova interview, http://www.pbs.org/wgbh/nova/physics/mandelbrot-fractal.html; his TED talk (http://www.ted.com/speakers/benoit_mandelbrot), and that of Ron Eglash (http://www.ted.com/talks/ron_eglash_on_african_fractals).

130 This entry owes much to the Numberphile video on transcendental numbers, narrated by Simon Pampena: https://www.youtube.com/watch?v=seUU2bZtfgM. Thanks to my mathematician friend Jonah Gaster, who first suggested transcendental numbers as a model of patternlessness and reviewed this entry. Tammet's description comes from Daniel Tammet, Born on a Blue Day: Inside the Extraordinary Mind of an Autistic Savant (Free Press, 2007), all of chapter 10 but especially pages 177–178. Tammet's most recent book, Thinking in Numbers (New York: Little, Brown and Company, 2013), explores his synesthesia and imaginative impressions about numbers in greater—and fascinating—detail.

A Note On The Author

Jude Stewart writes about design and culture for *Slate*, the *Believer*, and *Fast Company*, among others. A contributing editor for *PRINT*, she blogs about design for that magazine and AIGA. Her first book, *ROY G. BIV: An Exceedingly Surprising Book About Color*, was published by Bloomsbury in 2013. Read more at www.judestewart.com.